SECOND EDITION

Ruby Pocket Reference

Michael Fitzgerald

Beijing · Boston · Farnham · Sebastopol · Tokyo

Ruby Pocket Reference

by Michael Fitzgerald

Copyright © 2015 Michael Fitzgerald. All rights reserved.

Printed in the United States of America.

Published by O'Reilly Media, Inc., 1005 Gravenstein Highway North, Sebastopol, CA 95472.

O'Reilly books may be purchased for educational, business, or sales promotional use. Online editions are also available for most titles (*http://safaribooksonline.com*). For more information, contact our corporate/institutional sales department: 800-998-9938 or *corporate@oreilly.com*.

Editor: Brian MacDonald
Production Editors: Colleen Lobner and Nicole Shelby
Copyeditor: Gillian McGarvey
Proofreader: Kim Cofer
Indexer: WordCo Indexing Services
Interior Designer: David Futato
Cover Designer: Ellie Volckhausen
Illustrator: Rebecca Demarest

| July 2007: | First Edition |
| August 2015: | Second Edition |

Revision History for the Second Edition

2015-08-05: First Release

See *http://oreilly.com/catalog/errata.csp?isbn=9781491926017* for release details.

978-1-491-92601-7

[M]

Table of Contents

Ruby Pocket Reference

Introduction

Ruby is an open source, object-oriented scripting language created by Yukihiro "Matz" Matsumoto and initially released in Japan in 1995. Ruby has since gained worldwide acceptance as an easy-to-learn, powerful, and expressive programming language. An interpreted language, Ruby runs on all major platforms. For the latest information on Ruby, see *http://www.ruby-lang.org*. For online Ruby documentation, see *http://ruby-doc.org*.

This edition of the *Ruby Pocket Reference* supports version 2.2.2 of Ruby, the current version at the time of writing.

Conventions Used in This Book

The following typographical conventions are used in this book:

Italic

    Indicates new terms, URLs, email addresses, filenames, and file extensions.

`Constant width`

    Used for program listings, as well as within paragraphs to refer to program elements such as variable or function names, databases, data types, environment variables, statements, and keywords.

Constant width bold
> Shows commands or other text that should be typed literally by the user.

Constant width italic
> Shows text that should be replaced with user-supplied values or by values determined by context.

NOTE

This element signifies a general note.

Using Code Examples

Supplemental material (code examples, exercises, etc.) is available for download at *https://github.com/michaeljamesfitzgerald/Ruby-Pocket-Reference-2nd-Edition*.

This book is here to help you get your job done. In general, if example code is offered with this book, you may use it in your programs and documentation. You do not need to contact us for permission unless you're reproducing a significant portion of the code. For example, writing a program that uses several chunks of code from this book does not require permission. Selling or distributing a CD-ROM of examples from O'Reilly books does require permission. Answering a question by citing this book and quoting example code does not require permission. Incorporating a significant amount of example code from this book into your product's documentation does require permission.

We appreciate, but do not require, attribution. An attribution usually includes the title, author, publisher, and ISBN. For example: "*Ruby Pocket Reference, 2nd Edition* by Michael Fitzgerald (O'Reilly). Copyright 2015 Michael Fitzgerald, 978-1-4919-2601-7."

If you feel your use of code examples falls outside fair use or the permission given above, feel free to contact us at *permissions@oreilly.com*.

Safari® Books Online

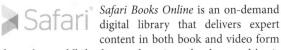 *Safari Books Online* is an on-demand digital library that delivers expert content in both book and video form from the world's leading authors in technology and business.

Technology professionals, software developers, web designers, and business and creative professionals use Safari Books Online as a primary resource for research, problem solving, learning, and certification training.

Safari Books Online offers a range of plans and pricing for enterprise, government, education, and individuals.

Members have access to thousands of books, training videos, and prepublication manuscripts in one fully searchable database from publishers like O'Reilly Media, Prentice Hall Professional, Addison-Wesley Professional, Microsoft Press, Sams, Que, Peachpit Press, Focal Press, Cisco Press, John Wiley & Sons, Syngress, Morgan Kaufmann, IBM Redbooks, Packt, Adobe Press, FT Press, Apress, Manning, New Riders, McGraw-Hill, Jones & Bartlett, Course Technology, and hundreds more. For more information about Safari Books Online, please visit us online.

How to Contact Us

Please address comments and questions concerning this book to the publisher:

O'Reilly Media, Inc.
1005 Gravenstein Highway North
Sebastopol, CA 95472
800-998-9938 (in the United States or Canada)
707-829-0515 (international or local)
707-829-0104 (fax)

We have a web page for this book, where we list errata, examples, and any additional information. You can access this page at *http://bit.ly/ruby-pocket-ref-2e*.

To comment or ask technical questions about this book, send email to *bookquestions@oreilly.com*.

For more information about our books, courses, conferences, and news, see our website at *http://www.oreilly.com*.

Find us on Facebook: *http://facebook.com/oreilly*

Follow us on Twitter: *http://twitter.com/oreillymedia*

Watch us on YouTube: *http://www.youtube.com/oreillymedia*

Acknowledgments

The second edition of this book is dedicated to the memory of my brother Mark S. Fitzgerald (1955–2012).

I want to thank Simon St. Laurent for helping to make this book happen and Brian MacDonald for his patient support while I wrote this new edition. I also want to thank my technical reviewers, Justin Page and Mike Korcynski, who essentially busted my technical chops. Thanks, guys.

Running Ruby

Test whether Ruby is available on your computer by typing the following at a command or shell prompt:

```
$ ruby --version
```

The response you get from this command should look similar to the following (if running Mac OS X Yosemite):

```
ruby 2.2.2p95 (2015-04-13 revision 50295)
  [x86_64-darwin14]
```

You can install Ruby on any of the major platforms—Windows, Mac, or flavors of Linux. For Ruby file archives and installation instructions, see *http://www.ruby-lang.org/en/downloads* and *https://www.ruby-lang.org/en/documentation/installation/*. To manage multiple versions of Ruby on a single computer, consider using Ruby Version Manager or RVM (*http://rvm.io*) or rbenv (*https://github.com/sstephenson/rbenv*). To easily and straightforwardly install the latest version of Ruby on a Mac, try Homebrew (*http://brew.sh*).

Running the Ruby Interpreter

View Ruby switches (command-line options) by entering:

```
$ ruby --help
```

Or, for a shorter message:

```
$ ruby -h
```

Usage:

```
ruby [switches] [--] [programfile] [arguments]
```

-0 [*octal*]
> Specify a record separator (\0 if no argument).

-a
> Autosplit mode with -n or -p (splits $_ into $F).

-c
> Check program syntax only (replies Syntax OK).

-C*directory*

    cd to directory before executing script.

-d [or] --debug

    Set debugging flags (sets predefined variable $DEBUG to true).

-e '*command*'

    Execute one line of script; more than one -e allowed; omit *programfile*.

-E*ex[:in]* **[or]** --encoding=*ex[:in]*

    Specify the default internal and external character encodings.

-F*pattern*

    split() pattern for autosplit (-a).

-i*extension*

    Edit ARGV files in place (make backup if optional extension supplied).

-I*directory*

    Specify $LOAD_PATH (predefined variable) directory; may be used more than once.

-l

    Enable line-ending processing.

-n

    Assume 'while gets(); ... end' loop around your script.

-p

    Assume loop like -n but print line also like sed.

-r*library*

    Require library before executing your script.

-s

    Enable some switch parsing for switches after script name.

`-S`

  Look for the script using PATH environment variable.

`-T[`*`level=1`*`]`

  Turn on tainting checks.

`-v` **[or]** `--verbose`

  Print version information, then turn on verbose mode (compare `--version`).

`-w`

  Turn on warnings for script.

`-W[`*`level=2`*`]`

  Set warning level: 0 = silence, 1 = medium, and 2 = verbose (default).

`-x[`*`directory`*`]`

  Strip off text before `#!` (shebang) line, and optionally `cd` to directory.

`--copyright`

  Print the Ruby copyright message.

`--enable=feature[, . . .]` **[or]** `--disable=feature[, . . .]`

  Enable or disable features. See "Features."

`--external-encoding=`*`encoding`* **[or]**

`--internal-encoding=`*`encoding`*

  Specify the default external or internal character encoding.

`--version`

  Print version information (compare `-v`).

`--help`

  Show this help message (compare `-h` [short message]).

Features:

`gems`

  Rubygems (default: enabled).

`rubyopt`

  RUBYOPT environment variable (default: enabled).

Interactive Ruby (irb)

Interactive Ruby, or irb, is an interactive programming environment that comes with Ruby. It was written by Keiju Ishitsuka. To invoke it, type irb at a shell or command prompt, and begin entering Ruby statements and expressions. Use exit or quit to exit. See *http://ruby-doc.org/stdlib-2.2.2/libdoc/irb/rdoc/index.html*.

Usage:

```
irb[.rb] [options] [programfile] [arguments]
```

For example, to get the current version of irb, use:

```
irb --version # => irb 0.9.6(09/06/30)
```

Options:

-f

   Suppress reading of the file ˜/.irbrc.

-m

   bc mode (mathn, fraction, or matrix available). [Note that mathn is deprecated as of 2.2.]

-d

   Set $DEBUG to true (same as ruby -d).

-r *load-module*
   Same as ruby -r.

-I *path*
   Specify $LOAD_PATH directory.

-U
   Same as ruby -U.

-E *enc*
   Same as ruby -E.

-w
   Same as ruby -w.

`-W[`*`level=2`*`]`
> Same as `ruby -W`.

`--context-mode `*`n`*
> Set n[*0–3*] to method to create binding object when new workspace created.

`--echo`
> Show result (default).

`--noecho`
> Don't show result.

`--inspect`
> Use `inspect` for output (default except for bc mode).

`--noinspect`
> Don't use `inspect` for output.

`--readline`
> Use Readline extension module.

`--noreadline`
> Don't use Readline extension module.

`--prompt `*`prompt-mode`*` (--prompt-mode `*`prompt-mode`*`)`
> Switch prompt mode. Predefined prompt modes are *default*, *simple*, *xmp*, and *inf-ruby*.

`--inf-ruby-mode`
> Use prompt appropriate for *inf-ruby-mode* on Emacs. Suppresses `--readline`.

`--sample-book-mode (--simple-prompt)`
> Simple prompt mode.

`--noprompt`
> No prompt mode.

`--single-irb`
> Share self with sub-irb.

`--tracer`

    Display trace for each execution of command.

`--back-trace-limit` *n*

    Display backtrace top *n* and tail *n*. The default value is 16.

`--irb_debug` *n*

    Set internal debug level to *n* (not commonly used).

`--verbose`

    Show details.

`--noverbose`

    Don't show details.

`-v` *(`--version`)*.

    Print the version of `irb`.

`-h` *(`--help`)*.

    Print help.

`--`

    Separate options of `irb` from list of command-line arguments.

Following is a sample of expressions evaluated by `irb`:

```
$ irb --noprompt
23 + 27
50
50 - 23
27
10 * 5
50
10**5
100000
50 / 5
10
x = 1
1
x + 59
60
hi = "Hello, Matz!"
"Hello, Matz!"
hi.each_char { |s| print s }
Hello, Matz!=> "Hello, Matz!"
```

```
1.upto( 10 ) { |n| print n, " " }
1 2 3 4 5 6 7 8 9 10 => 1
100 < 1_000
true
class Hello
attr :hi, true
end
nil
h = Hello.new
#<Hello:0x3602cc>
h.hi = "Hello, Matz!"
"Hello, Matz!"
h.hi
"Hello, Matz!"
self
main
self.class
Object
exit # or quit
```

You can also invoke a single program with irb. After running
the program, irb exits:

```
$ cat hello.rb
#!/usr/bin/env ruby

class Hello
 def initialize( hello )
 @hello = hello
 end
 def hello
 @hello
 end
end

salute = Hello.new( "Hello, Matz!" )
puts salute.hello
$ irb hello.rb
hello.rb(main):001:0> #!/usr/bin/env ruby
hello.rb(main):002:0*
hello.rb(main):003:0* class Hello
hello.rb(main):004:1>  def initialize( hello )
hello.rb(main):005:2>    @hello = hello
hello.rb(main):006:2>  end
hello.rb(main):007:1>  def hello
hello.rb(main):008:2>    @hello
hello.rb(main):009:2>  end
hello.rb(main):010:1> end
```

```
=> nil
hello.rb(main):011:0>
hello.rb(main):012:0* salute = Hello.new( "Hello,
  Matz!" )
=> #<Hello:0x007fd28b036f50 @hello="Hello, Matz!">
=> #<Hello:0x319f20 @hello="Hello, Matz!">
hello.rb(main):013:0> puts salute.hello
Hello, Matz!
=> nil
hello.rb(main):014:0> $
```

When running any code that follows in this book, you can run it either in irb or with the Ruby interpreter, unless another one is specified.

Using a Shebang Comment on Unix/Linux

Use a shebang comment on the first line of a Ruby program to help a Unix/Linux system execute the commands in a program file according to a specified interpreter, Ruby. Keep in mind that this does not work on Windows. Listed here is a very short program named *hi.rb* with a shebang on the first line:

```
#!/usr/bin/env ruby

puts "Hi, world!"
```

Other possible shebang lines or comments are #!/usr/bin/ruby -w (warnings on) or #!/usr/local/bin/ruby. The location of the Ruby executable could vary given that you might be using a version manager like RVM and rbenv. With a shebang in place, you can type the name of the executable script, followed by Return or Enter, at a shell prompt without invoking the Ruby interpreter directly:

```
$ ./hello.rb
```

TIP

Make sure the file is executable with chmod +x.

Associating File Types on Windows

Windows doesn't know or care about a shebang comment (#!), but you can achieve a similar result by creating a file type association with the `assoc` and `ftype` commands on Windows (DOS). To find out whether an association exists for the file extension *.rb*, use the `assoc` command:

```
C:\Ruby Code>assoc .rb
File association not found for extension .rb
```

If it's not found, associate the *.rb* extension with a file type like this:

```
C:\Ruby Code>assoc .rb=rbFile
```

Then test again whether the association exists:

```
C:\Ruby Code>assoc .rb
.rb=rbFile
```

Now test to see whether the file type for Ruby exists with `ftype`:

```
C:\Ruby Code>ftype rbfile
File type 'rbfile' not found or no open command
  associated with it.
```

If not found, you can create it with a command like this, depending on where Ruby is located on your machine:

```
C:\Ruby Code>ftype rbfile="C:\Program Files\Ruby\bin
\ruby.exe" "%1" %*
```

Be sure to put the correct path to the executable for the Ruby interpreter, followed by the substitution variables. `%1` is a substitution variable for the file you want to run; `%*` accepts all other parameters that may appear on the command line. Test it:

```
C:\Ruby Code>ftype rbfile rbfile="C:\Program Files\Ruby
\bin\ruby.exe" "%1" %*
```

Finally, add *.rb* to the `PATHEXT` environment variable. See whether it is there already with `set`:

```
C:\Ruby Code>set PATHEXT
PATHEXT=.COM;.EXE;.BAT;.CMD;.VBS;.VBE;.JS;.JSE;
  .WSF;.WSH;.tcl
```

If it is not there, add it like this:

```
C:\Ruby Code>set PATHEXT=.rb;%PATHEXT%
```

Then test again:

```
C:\Ruby Code>set PATHEXT
PATHEXT=.rb;.COM;.EXE;.BAT;.CMD;.VBS;.VBE;.JS;.JSE;
  .WSF;.WSH;.tcl
```

All is now in order:

```
C:\Ruby Code>type hi.rb
#!/usr/bin/env ruby

puts "Hi, World!"
```

Make sure you are able to execute the file:

```
C:\Ruby Code>cacls hi.rb /g username:f
Are you sure (Y/N)?y
processed file: C:\Ruby Code\hi.rb
```

Run the program by entering the program's filename at the command prompt, with or without the file extension:

```
C:\Ruby Code>hi
Hi, World!
```

To preserve these settings, you can add these commands to your *autoexec.bat* file, or set the environment variables by selecting **Start** → **Control Panel** → **System**, clicking the **Advanced** tab, and then clicking the **Environment Variables** button.

Ruby's Keywords

Table 1 contains a list of Ruby's keywords (also known as *reserved words*).

Table 1. Ruby's keywords

Keyword	Description
BEGIN	Code, enclosed in braces ({ }), to run *before* the program runs.

Keyword	Description
END	Code, enclosed in braces ({ }), to run *after* the program ends.
alias	Creates an alias for an existing method. See also Module#alias_method.
and	Logical operator; same as && except and has lower precedence.
begin	Begins a code block or group of statements; closes with end.
break	Terminates a while or until loop, or a method inside a block.
case	Compares an expression with a matching when clause; closes with end. See also when.
class	Begins class definition; closes with end.
def	Begins method definition; closes with end.
defined?	A special operator that determines whether a variable, method, super method, or block exists.
do	Begins a block, then executes code in that block; closes with end.
else	Executes following code if previous conditional is not true; used with if, elsif, unless, or case. See if, elsif.
elsif	Executes following code if previous conditional is not true; used with if or another elsif.
end	Ends a code block (group of statements) started with begin, class, def, do, if, etc.
ensure	Always executes at block termination; use after last rescue.
false	Logical or Boolean false; singleton; instance of False Class; a keyword literal. See true.
for	Begins a for loop; used with in.
if	Executes code block if conditional statement is true. Closes with end. Compare unless, until.

Keyword	Description
in	Used with for loop. See for.
module	Begins module definition; closes with end.
next	Jumps to the point immediately before the evaluation of the loop's conditional. Compare redo.
nil	Empty, uninitialized, or invalid; always false, but not the same as zero; singleton; instance of NilClass; a keyword literal.
not	Logical operator; same as !.
or	Logical operator; same as || except or has lower precedence.
redo	Restarts current iteration, transferring control back to top of loop or iterator. Compare to next.
rescue	Evaluates an expression after an exception is raised; used before ensure.
retry	Inside rescue, jumps to top of block (begin). Iterator restart deprecated as of 1.9.
return	Returns a value from a method or block. May be omitted, but method and block always return a value, whether explicit or not.
self	Evaluates to the current object; a keyword literal.
super	Calls method of the same name in the superclass. The *superclass* is the parent of this class.
then	Separator used with if, unless, when, case, and rescue. May be omitted, unless conditional is all on one line.
true	Logical or Boolean true; singleton; instance of TrueClass; a keyword variable. See false.
undef	Undefines a method in the current class.
unless	Executes code block if conditional statement is false. Compare if and until.

Keyword	Description
until	Executes code block while conditional statement is `false`. Compare `if` and `unless`.
when	Starts a clause (one or more) under `case`. See `case`.
while	Executes code while the conditional statement is `true`.
yield	Executes the block passed to a method.
__ENCODING__	Current character encoding (object of `Encoding` class); a keyword literal.
__FILE__	Name (string) of current source file; a keyword literal.
__LINE__	Number (integer) of current line in the current source file; a keyword literal.

Ruby's Operators

Table 2 lists all of Ruby's operators in descending order of precedence. Operators that are implemented as methods may be overridden and are indicated in the Method? column with a checkmark (✓).

Table 2. Ruby's operators

Operator	Description	Method?
! ~ +	Boolean NOT, bitwise complement, unary plus	✓
**	Exponentiation	✓
-	Unary minus	✓
* / %	Multiplication, division, modulo (remainder)	✓
+ -	Addition (or concatenation), subtraction	✓
<< >>	Bitwise shift-left (append), bitwise shift-right	✓
&	Bitwise AND	✓

Operator	Description	Method?
| ^	Bitwise OR, bitwise exclusive OR	✓
> >= < <=	Greater than, greater than or equal to, less than, less than or equal to	✓
<=> == === != =~ !~	Equality comparison (spaceship, equality, equality, not equal to, match, not match)	✓
&&	Boolean AND	
||	Boolean OR	
.. ...	Range inclusive (..), range exclusive (...)	✓ (not ...)
? :	Ternary (acts like compact if/then/else)	
= += -= *= /= %= **= <<= >>= &= |= ^= &&=	Assignment (=), abbreviated assignment (all others)	
not	Logical negation	
and or	Logical composition	
defined?	Tests variable definition and type	

The following trivial program, *over_op.rb*, shows one way to override the definition for the unary operator -. The at sign (@) lets the interpreter know that the operator is unary, not binary. Once overridden, the operator will convert the string str to a symbol—not particularly useful, but you get the idea.

```
str = "Matz"

def str.-@
  to_sym
end

p -str # :Matz
```

Here is a slightly less trivial version using a class. See "Classes" on page 51.

```
class MyString < String

  def -@
    to_sym
  end

end

str = MyString.new "Matz"

p -str # :Matz
```

Comments

A comment hides a line of code, part of a line of code, or multiple lines of code from the Ruby interpreter, either by using the hash or pound character (#), or =begin and =end. Create a comment by using a hash character at the beginning of a line:

```
# I'm a comment. Ignore me.
```

Or a comment may follow a statement or expression, hiding part of a line:

```
first_name = "Matsumoto" # Or given name
```

You can use hash characters to hide several lines together:

```
# This is a comment.
# This is another comment.
# This is yet another comment.
# Okay. That's enough.
```

Or you can hide multiple lines using the =begin/=end syntax:

```
=begin
This is a comment.
This is a comment, too.
This is a comment, too.
I said that already.
=end
```

Numbers

Numbers are not primitives in Ruby as in other languages; each number in Ruby is an object, an instance of one of Ruby's core numeric classes.

- `Numeric` is Ruby's base class for numbers. The `Integer` class is the basis for two concrete classes that hold whole numbers: `Fixnum` and `Bignum`.
- `Fixnum` is used for fixed-length numbers (integers) with the bit length of the native machine word, minus 1, whereas `Bignum` holds integers outside the range of `Fixnum`.
- A `Bignum` is created automatically if an operation or assignment yields a result too large for `Fixnum`; the only limitation on the size of integer `Bignum` can represent is the available memory.
- The `Float` class is for floating-point numbers. It is the native architecture's double-precision floating-point representation internally.
- The `Complex` class represents complex numbers—that is, a number expressed in the form $a+bi$ where i is an imaginary number (or unit). Once a part of the standard library, `Complex` is now in Ruby's core.
- `Rational` represents rational numbers—that is, the quotient of two integers in the form a/b. Now part of Ruby's core.

Here are several numeric classes from the standard library. Before you can use these, you must `require` code from the standard library using, for example, `require 'matrix'`. For more details, see `Kernel#require` at *http://ruby-doc.org/core-2.2.2/Kernel.html* or type `ri Kernel#require` at a shell prompt. `Kernel` is a Ruby module that's included in the `Object` class, making its methods available to all Ruby programs.

- BigDecimal provides arbitrary precision for very large or very accurate floating-point decimal arithmetic. Its parent class is Numeric.
- The Matrix class represents mathematical matrices, providing methods for creating matrices, operating on them, and determining their properties. Its parent is Object.

Table 3 lists some numeric examples.

Table 3. Ruby's numbers and their associated types

Number	Description
2411	Integer, of class Fixnum.
2_411	Integer, of class Fixnum (underscore ignored).
2411.0	Float, of class Float.
0.2411E4	Scientific notation, of class BigDecimal.
04553	Octal, of class Fixnum.
0x96b	Hexadecimal, of class Fixnum.
0b100101101011	Binary, of class Fixnum.
24110000000000000000	Integer, of class Bignum.
(2411+2i)	Complex number, result of Complex(2411,2).
2411i	i suffix converts to complex (2411/1).
(2/1)	Rational number, result of Rational(2411,1205.5).
2411r	r suffix converts to rational (0+2411i).
2411ri	ri suffix converts to (0+(2411/1)*i).

Figure 1 shows a hierarchy of Ruby's math classes.

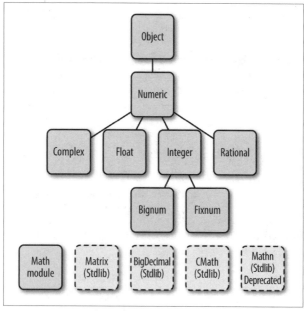

Figure 1. Hierarchy of Ruby math classes

Variables

A variable is an identifier that is assigned to an object, and which may hold a value. Ruby variables are not declared, nor are they statically typed. Instead, the type of value is assigned at runtime. Ruby uses *duck typing*, which is a kind of dynamic typing. If a value behaves or acts like a certain type (duck), such as an integer, Ruby gives it a context and treats it as such (it's probably a duck). If a variable is able to act like an integer, for example, then it is legal and appropriate to use it in that context.

Local Variables

A *local variable* has a local scope or context. If defined within a method, for example, its scope is kept within that method. Local variable names must begin with either a lowercase letter or an underscore (_), and must not be prefixed with @, @@, or $ because they are reserved for other types of variables. Following are a few examples of local variables:

```
x = 1.0    # x is a Float
y = "Yes"  # y is a String
_temp = 16 # _temp is a Fixnum
```

Instance Variables

An *instance variable* belongs to a particular instance of a class, hence the name. It can only be accessed from outside that instance via an accessor (helper) method. Instance variables are always prefixed with a single at sign (@), as in @hello. See "Classes" on page 51.

Class Variables

A *class variable* is shared among all instances of a class. Only one copy of a class variable exists for a given class. It is prefixed by two at signs (@@), such as @@times. You have to initialize (declare a value for) a class variable before you use it. See "Classes" on page 51.

Global Variables

Global variables are globally available to a program, inside any structure. Their scope is the whole program. They are prefixed by a dollar sign ($), such as $amount. Matz's opinion of global variables is, and I quote, "They are ugly, so don't use them." Take his advice. Use singletons instead. See "Singletons" on page 57.

A global variable may be aliased with the keyword `alias`, as shown in this simple example (*alias_global.rb*):

```
$a = 100
alias $b $a
puts $b # => 100
```

Constants

Constant names must begin with a capital letter (Matz) and by convention frequently use all capitals (MATZ), making them easy to spot. Class names, for example, are constants. As their name suggests, constants are not expected to have their values changed after initial assignment. You can reassign a value to a constant, but Ruby will generate a warning if you do. Second, and more importantly, since constants refer to objects, the contents of the object *to which the constant refers* might change without Ruby generating a warning. Thus, Ruby constants are called *mutable* because although a constant is only expected to refer to a single object throughout the program, the value of that object may vary. Finally, constants must have a value assigned to them to exist.

Parallel Variable Assignment

With parallel assignment, you can assign several values to several variables in a single expression, based on order. A list of variables, separated by commas, can be placed to the left of the equals sign, with the list of values to assign them on the right. Here are a few examples:

```
x, y, z = 100, 200, 500
a, b, c = "cash", 1.99, 100
```

Symbols

Ruby has a special object called a *symbol*. Symbols are like placeholders for identifiers and strings. They are always prefixed by a colon (:); for example, :en and :logos. Only one copy of the symbol is held in a single memory address as long as the program is running. You don't create a symbol directly by assigning a value to it. You create a symbol by calling the String#to_sym or String#intern methods on a string, or by assigning a symbol to a symbol:

```
name = "Bobby"
name.to_sym # => :Bobby
name.intern # => :Bobby
"Hello".to_sym # => :Hello
:Hello.to_s # => "Hello"
:Hello.id2name # => "Hello"
name == :Bobby.to_s # => true
hash = { :lang1 => :English, :lang2 => :German,
  :lang3 => :French }
```

For more information, see *http://ruby-doc.org/core-2.2.2/ Symbol.html*.

Predefined Global Variables

Table 4 lists Ruby's predefined global variables. To generate a list of these variables with Ruby, invoke the following at a command prompt:

```
ruby -e 'puts global_variables.sort'
```

Or in a program, iterate over the globals with each (to yield symbols):

```
global_variables.sort.each { |name| p name }
```

Kernel#p writes one or more objects to standard output, followed by a newline, à la *object*.inspect.

Table 4. Predefined global variables

Global variable	Description
$!	The exception information message containing the last exception raised. raise sets this variable. Access with => in a rescue clause. The Exception#cause method, available since 2.1, also returns this information.
$@	The stack backtrace (array) of the last exception, retrievable via Exception#backtrace.

Global variable	Description
$&	The string matched by the last successful pattern match in this scope, or nil if the last pattern match failed. Same as m[0] where m is a MatchData object. Read only. Local.
$`	String preceding (to the left of) whatever was matched by the last successful pattern match in the current scope, or nil if the last pattern match failed. Same as m.pre_match where m is a MatchData object. Read only. Local.
$'	String following (to the right of) whatever was matched by the last successful pattern match in the current scope, or nil if the last pattern match failed. Same as m.post_match where m is a MatchData object. Read only. Local.
$+	Last bracket (highest group) matched by the last successful search pattern, or nil if the last pattern match failed. Useful if you don't know which of a set of alternative patterns matched. Read only. Local.
$1, $2, . . .	Subpattern from the corresponding set of parentheses in the last successful pattern matched, not counting patterns matched in nested blocks that have been exited already, or nil if the last pattern match failed. Same as m[n] where m is a MatchData object. Read only. Local.
$~	Information about the last match in the current scope. Regex#match returns the last match information. Setting this variable affects match variables like $&, $+, $1, $2, etc. The nth subexpression can be retrieved by $~[nth]. Local.
$=	Case-insensitive flag; nil by default. Deprecated in 1.9.
$/	Input record separator, newline by default. Works like awk's RS variable. If it is set to nil, a whole file will be read at once. gets, readline, etc. take the input record separator as an optional argument. See also $-0.

Global variable	Description
$\	Output record separator for print and IO#write; nil by default.
$,	Output field separator between arguments; also the default separator for Array#join, which allows you to indicate a separator explicitly.
$;	The default separator for String#split; nil by default. See also $-F
$.	The current input line number of the last file that was read. Same as ARGF.lineno.
$<	The virtual concatenation file of the files given by command-line arguments, or standard input (in case no argument file is supplied). $<.filename returns the current filename. Alias for ARGF.
$>	Default output for print; printf, $stdout by default. Alias for $defout.
$_	Last input line of string by gets or readline in the current scope; set to nil if gets or readline meets EOF. Local.
$0	Name of the current Ruby program being executed.
$*	Command-line arguments given for the script, with options (arguments) for the Ruby interpreter removed.
$$	Process number (process.pid) of the Ruby program being executed.
$?	Exit status of the last executed child process.
$:	Load path for scripts and binary modules by Kernel#load or Kernel#require. Alias for $LOAD_PATH; see also $-l.
$"	Array containing the module names loaded by Kernel#require. Used to prevent require from loading modules twice. Compare $LOADED_FEATURES.

Global variable	Description
$DEBUG	True if -d or --debug switch is set. Prints each exception raised to $stderr (but not its backtrace). Setting this to true enables debug output as if -d were given on the command line; setting to false disables debug output. See also $-d.
$LOADED_ FEATURES	Array containing the module names loaded by Kernel#require. Used for preventing require from loading modules twice. Compare $".
$FILENAME	Name of the file currently being read from ARGF ($<). Same as ARGF.filename or $<.filename.
$LOAD_PATH	Load path for scripts and binary modules by Kernel#load or Kernel#require. Alias for $: and $-I.
$stderr	The current standard error output; STDERR by default.
$stdin	The current standard input; STDIN by default.
$stdout	The current standard output; STDOUT by default.
$VERBOSE	True if verbose flag is set by -v, -w, or --verbose switches; nil disables warnings, including those from Kernel#warn.
$-0	Input record separator, newline by default. Works like awk's RS variable. If set to nil, a whole file will be read at once. gets, readline, etc. take the input record separator as an optional argument. Alias of $/.
$-a	True if option -a is set. Read-only.
$-d	True if -d or --debug switch is set. Prints each exception raised to $stderr (but not its backtrace). Setting this to true enables debug output as if -d were given on the command line; setting to false disables debug output. Alias of $DEBUG.
$-F	The default separator for String#split; nil by default. Alias of $;.

Global variable	Description
`$-i`	In in-place-edit mode, this variable holds the extension, otherwise `nil`. Can enable or disable in-place-edit mode.
`$-I`	Load path for scripts and binary modules by `Kernel#load` or `Kernel#require`. Alias for `$:` and `$LOAD_PATH`.
`$-l`	True if option `-l` is set (enable line-ending processing). Read-only.
`$-p`	True if option `-p` is set (which assumes loop like `-n` but prints line also, like `sed`). Read-only.
`$-v` [or] `$-w`	True if verbose flag is set by `-v`, `-w`, or `--verbose` switches; `nil` disables warnings, including those from `Kernel#warn`. Alias for `$VERBOSE`.

Keyword Literals

Table 5 shows Ruby's *keyword literals*, which are objects that look like a variable, act like a constant, and can't be assigned a value.

Table 5. Keyword literals

Keyword Literal	Description
`false`	Logical or Boolean false; singleton; instance of `False Class`. See also `true`.
`nil`	Empty, uninitialized, or invalid; always `false`, but not the same as zero; singleton; instance of `NilClass`.
`self`	Evaluates to the current object.
`true`	Logical or Boolean `true`; singleton; instance of `True Class`. See `false`.
`__ENCODING__`	Current character encoding (object of `Encoding` class).
`__FILE__`	Name (string) of current source file.
`__LINE__`	Number (integer) of current line in the current source file.

Global Constants

Table 6 describes all of Ruby's global constants.

Table 6. Global constants

Global Constant	Description
ARGF	I/O-like stream that allows access to a virtual concatenation of all files provided on the command line, or standard input if no files are provided. Alias for $<.
ARGV	Array that contains all the command-line arguments passed to a program. Alias for $*.
DATA	An input stream for reading the lines of code following the __END__ directive. Not defined if __END__ is not present in code.
ENV	A hash-like object containing the program's environment variables; can be treated as a hash.
FALSE	Alias for false; false is preferred.
NIL	Alias for nil; nil is preferred.
PLATFORM	Alias for RUBY_PLATFORM. Deprecated.
RELEASE_DATE	Alias for RUBY_RELEASE_DATE. Deprecated.
RUBY_PLATFORM	A string indicating the platform of the Ruby interpreter; for example, "x86_64-darwin14."
RUBY_RELEASE_DATE	A string indicating the release date of the Ruby interpreter; for example, "2014-12-25."
RUBY_VERSION	The Ruby version; for example, "2.2.2."
STDERR	Standard error output stream with default value of $stderr.
STDIN	Standard input stream with default value of $stdin.
STDOUT	Standard output stream with default value of $stdout.
TOPLEVEL_BINDING	A Binding object at Ruby's top level.

Global Constant	Description
TRUE	Alias for true; true is preferred.
VERSION	Alias for RUBY_VERSION. Deprecated.

Ranges

A *range* is an interval or set of values. Ruby supports ranges using the operators .. (inclusive) and ... (exclusive). The range 1..12, for example, includes all the numbers in the range, 1 through 12; however, in the range 1...12, the ending value 12 is excluded.

The === method determines whether a value is a member of or included in a range:

```
(1..25) === 14 # => true, in range
(1..25) === 26 # => false, out of range
(1...25) === 25 # => false, out of range
  (used ...)
```

You can use a range to create an array of digits:

```
(1..9).to_a # => [1, 2, 3, 4, 5, 6, 7, 8, 9]
```

You can also create an inclusive range like this:

```
digits = Range.new(1, 9)
digits.to_a # => [1, 2, 3, 4, 5, 6, 7, 8, 9]
```

Or an exclusive range like this:

```
digits = Range.new(1,9,true)
digits.to_a # => [1, 2, 3, 4, 5, 6, 7, 8]
```

For more information, see *http://ruby-doc.org/core-2.2.2/ Range.html*.

NOTE

A *flip-flop expression* is an obscure use of a range operator. For example, `(1..7).each {|n| p n if n==2..n>=5}` prints 2 through 5. A flip-flop expression is `false` until the expression on the left evaluates to `true`. It remains `true` until the expression on the right evaluates to `true`, and then goes back to `false`. Got that? Flip-flops came to Ruby by way of Perl, *sed*, and *awk*. They should generally be avoided but are worth a mention for the intrepid out there who will use them all the time.

Methods

Methods provide a way to collect and organize program statements and expressions into one place so that you can use them conveniently and repeatedly. Most of Ruby's operators are actually methods. Here is a simple definition of a method named `hello`, created with the keywords `def` and `end`:

```
def hello
 puts "Hello, world!"
end
```

When you invoke the method `hello`, it outputs or emits a string:

```
hello # => Hello, world!
```

You can undefine a method with `undef`:

```
undef hello # undefines the method named hello
hello # try calling this method now
NameError: undefined local variable or method
   'hello' for main:Object
```

Methods might or might not have parameters. The `repeat` method, inane as it is, takes two parameters, `word` and `times`:

```
def repeat( word, times )
 puts word * times
end
```

```
repeat("Hello! ", 3) # => Hello! Hello! Hello!
repeat "Goodbye! ", 4 # => Goodbye! Goodbye!
   Goodbye! Goodbye!
```

Parentheses are optional in most Ruby method definitions and calls; however, if you call a method within a method—a nested call—it might cause some confusion, both on the part of the coder and the Ruby interpreter. When using parentheses, keep in mind that the opening parenthesis must follow the method name with no intervening space.

For more information, see *http://ruby-doc.org/core-2.2.2/doc/syntax/methods_rdoc.html*.

For the purposes of this book, *parameters* are part of the method definition or signature, and *arguments* are the values passed by those parameters. I say this because sometimes parameters and arguments are used interchangeably.

NOTE

You may join an object and its method with either :: or ., but usually :: is used with class methods. You may also use # with instance methods.

Block Arguments

Blocks are namelessly passed to their associated methods. However, you can pass blocks to methods directly by using a *block argument*, which essentially turns them into named blocks. (No exception is generated if the block is not passed.) The block parameter must be the last parameter in the method definition and must be prefixed with an ampersand, as in &b. Because the value of the block argument is actually a Proc object, you have to use the Proc#call method rather than yield to process the block. Here's a sample (*block_arg.rb*):

```
def my_iterator(x, &b)
   i = 0
```

```
    while(i < x)
      b.call(i*x) # Use call with block parameter
      i += 1
    end
  end

  my_iterator(12) {|x| print x.to_s + " "}
  # => 0 12 24 36 48 60 72 84 96 108 120 132
```

Return Values

Methods have return values. In other languages, you explicitly return a value with a `return` statement. In Ruby, the value of the last expression evaluated is returned, *with or without* an explicit `return` statement. This is a Ruby idiom. You can also define a return value explicitly with the `return` keyword:

```
def hello
 return "Hello, world!"
end
```

Method Name Conventions

Ruby has conventions about the last character in method names. These conventions are very common but not enforced by the language. If a method name ends with a question mark (?), such as `eql?`, it means that the method returns a Boolean (`true` or `false`). For example:

```
x = 1.0
y = 1.0
x.eql? y # => true
```

If a method name ends in an exclamation point (!), like `delete!`, it indicates that the method is destructive, meaning it makes what are called *in place* changes to an object rather than to a copy—that is, it changes the object itself. You can see the difference in the result of the `String` methods `delete` and `delete!`:

```
der_mensch = "Matz!" # => "Matz!"
der_mensch.delete( "!" ) # => "Matz"
puts der_mensch # => Matz!
```

Aliasing Methods

Ruby has two ways to alias methods. The alias keyword creates method aliases, though such aliases are lexically scoped. You can also use the method Module#alias_method. Its result will be its value at runtime.

With the alias keyword, you create a copy of the method with a new method name, though both method invocations will point to the same object. The following example illustrates how to create an alias for the method greet with the keyword alias (*alias_key.rb*):

```ruby
def greet
  "Hi"
end
alias hi greet # alias greet as hi
hi # => "Hi"
```

A call to alias_method, a private instance method of the Module module, looks like this (*alias_method.rb*):

```ruby
class Greeting
  def greet
    "Hi"
  end
  alias_method :hi, :greet # alias greet as hi
end
puts Greeting.new.hi # => "Hi"
```

Blocks

A *block* in Ruby is more than just a code block or group of statements. A Ruby block is always invoked in conjunction with a method. Blocks, in fact, are closures, sometimes referred to as *nameless functions*. They work like methods within other methods that share variables with their outer methods. In Ruby, the closure or block is wrapped by braces ({}) or by do/end, and depends on the associated method (such as each) to do its work.

Here is a simple call to a block with the method each from Array:

```
pacific = [ "Washington", "Oregon", "California" ]

pacific.each do |element|
 puts element
end
```

The name within the bars (|element|) can be any name you want. The block uses it as a local variable to keep track of every element in the array, and later uses it to perform something with the element. You can replace do/end with a pair of braces, as is most commonly done. The braces actually have a higher precedence than do/end:

```
pacific.each { |e| puts e }
```

Be aware that if you use a variable name that already exists in the containing scope, the block assigns that variable each successive value, which might not be what you want. It does not generate a local variable to the block with that name, as you might expect. Thus, you get this behavior:

```
j = 7
(1..4).to_a.each { | j | } # j now equals 4
```

The yield statement

A yield statement executes a block associated with a method. For example, this gimme method contains nothing more than a yield statement:

```
def gimme
 yield
end
```

To find out what yield does, call gimme and see what happens:

```
gimme
LocalJumpError: no block given
 from (irb):11:in 'gimme'
 from (irb):13
 from :0
```

You get an error here because yield's job is to execute the code block that is associated with the method. That was missing in the call to gimme. We can avoid this error by using the Kernel#block_given? method. Redefine gimme with an if statement:

```
def gimme
 if block_given?
   yield
 else
   puts "I'm blockless!"
 end
end
```

Try it again with and without a block:

```
gimme { print "Say hi to the people." } # => Say hi to the
people.

gimme # => I'm blockless!
```

Redefine gimme to contain two yields, and then call it with a block:

```
def gimme
 if block_given?
   yield
   yield
 else
   puts "I'm blockless!"
 end
end

gimme { print "Say hi again. " } # => Say hi again.
  Say hi again.
```

Another thing you should know is that after yield executes, control comes back to the next statement immediately following yield.

Procs

Ruby lets you store *procs* (procedures) as first-class objects, complete with context. Because a proc is a first-class object, it can do things that other first-class objects can do—be created at runtime, stored in data structures, passed as parameters, and so forth.

You can create procs in several ways—with `Proc::new` or by calling either the `Kernel#lambda` or `Kernel#proc` methods. Here are some lightweight examples (*proc.rb*). Note the lambda literal syntax, available since 1.9:

```
count = Proc.new { [1,2,3,4,5].each do |i| print i
  end; puts }
your_proc = lambda { puts "Lurch: 'You rang?'" }
other_proc = ->{ puts "Hmmmmm." } # new syntax
my_proc = proc { puts "Morticia: 'Who was at the
  door, Lurch?'" }

# What kind of objects did you just create?
p count.class # => Proc
p your_proc.class # => Proc
p other_proc.class # => Proc
p my_proc.class # => Proc

# Calling all procs
count.call # => 12345
your_proc.call # => Lurch: 'You rang?'
other_proc.call # => Hmmmmm.
my_proc.call # => Morticia: 'Who was at the door,
  Lurch?'
```

In addition, with the new lambda literal syntax for blocks, you replace the method name `lambda` with `->`, move arguments just before the braces, and use parentheses instead of a pair of parallel bars (|). For example:

```
y = ->(x){x+1}
```

Also, you can call the method `lambda?` to test whether an object is a lambda or not:

```
other_proc.lambda? # => true
my_proc.lambda? # => false
```

You can convert a block passed as a method argument to a `Proc` object by preceding the argument name with an ampersand (&) as follows:

```
def return_block
 yield
end

def return_proc( &proc )
 yield
end

return_block { puts "Got block!" }
return_proc {puts "Got block, convert to proc!"}
```

The method `return_block` has no arguments; all it has in its
body is a `yield` statement. The `yield` statement's purpose, once
again, is to execute a block when the block is passed to a
method. The next method, `return_proc`, has one argument,
`&proc`. When a method has an argument preceded by an
ampersand, it accepts the block, when one is submitted, and
converts it to a `Proc` object. With `yield` in the body, the method
executes the block *cum* proc, without having to bother with the
`Proc call` method.

Conditional Statements

A conditional statement tests whether a statement is `true` or
`false` and performs logic based on the answer. Both `true` and
`false` are keyword literals—you can't assign values to them.
The former is an object of `TrueClass`, and the latter is an object
of `FalseClass`.

Flow Control

For convenience, Table 7 lists Ruby's flow control statements,
most of which are used with conditionals.

Table 7. Flow control statements

Keyword or method	Description
break	Exits a loop or iterator.
catch	Kernel#catch executes a block, usually together with Kernel#throw. Used with exception handling.

Keyword or method	Description
next	Skips current iteration, moves to next.
redo	Restarts loop or iterator from beginning.
retry	Reexecutes block in rescue clause; however, iterator restart deprecated in 1.9.
return	Returns value and exits.
throw	Kernel#throw transfers control to catch block. Used with exception handling.

The if Statement

These three statements, each with a different form, begin with the keyword if and close with end:

```
if x == y then puts "x equals y" end

if x != y: puts "x is not equal to y" end

if x > y
 puts "x is greater than y"
end
```

The separator then (and its alias :, deprecated since 1.9) is optional unless the statement is on one line.

Negation

The negation operator ! reverses the true/false value of its expression:

```
if !x == y then puts "x does not equal y" end

if !x > y
 puts "x is not greater than y"
end
```

Multiple tests

Combine multiple tests in an if statement using && and ||, or their synonyms and and or, which have lower precedence:

```
ruby = "nifty"
programming = "fun"

if ruby == "nifty" && programming == "fun"
 puts "Keep programming!"
end

if a == 10 && b == 27 && c == 43 && d == -14
 print sum = a + b + c + d
end

if ruby=="nifty" and programming=="fun" and
   weather=="nice"
   puts "Stop programming and go outside!"
end

if a == 10 || b == 27 || c = 43 || d = -14
 print sum = a + b + c + d
end

if ruby == "nifty" or programming == "fun"
 puts "Keep programming!"
end
```

Statement modifier for if

You can also use if as a statement modifier by placing the if at the end of the statement:

```
puts "x is less than y" if x < y
```

The else statement

Add an optional else to execute a statement when if is not true:

```
if x >= y
 puts "x greater than or equal to y"
else
 puts "x is not greater than or equal to y"
end
```

The elsif statement

Use one or more optional elsif statements to test multiple statements (ending with an optional else, which must be last):

```
if x == y
 puts "x equals y"
elsif x != y
 puts "x is not equal to y"
elsif x > y
 puts "x is greater than y"
elsif x < y
 puts "x is less than y"
elsif x >= y
 puts "x is greater than or equal to y"
elsif x <= y
 puts "x is less than or equal to y"
else
 puts "Well, for the love of Pete"
end
```

The unless Statement

An unless statement is a negated form of the if statement.
Here is the first example of unless:

```
unless lang == "de"
 dog = "dog"
else
 dog = "Hund"
end
```

That first example is a negated form of the following if statement, and both examples accomplish the same thing:

```
if lang == "de"
 dog = "Hund"
else
 dog = "dog"
end
```

This example is saying, in effect, that unless the value of lang is
de, dog will be assigned the value of dog; otherwise, assign dog
the value Hund.

Statement modifier for unless

As with if, you can also use unless elegantly as a statement
modifier:

```
puts num += 1 unless num > 88
```

The while Statement

A while loop executes the code it contains as long as its conditional statement remains true:

```
i = 0
breeds = [ "quarter", "arabian", "appaloosa",
  "paint" ]
puts breeds.size # => 4
temp = []

while i < breeds.size do
 temp << breeds[i].capitalize
 i +=1
end

temp.sort! # => ["Appaloosa", "Arabian", "Paint", "Quarter"]
breeds.replace( temp )
p breeds # => ["Appaloosa", "Arabian", "Paint", "Quarter"]
```

The do keyword is optional. Once again, the method Kernel#p writes objects to standard output, followed by a newline.

You can also use begin and end with while, where the code in the loop is evaluated before the conditional is checked (like do/ while in C):

```
temp = 98.3

begin
 print "Your temperature is " + "%.1f" % temp +
  " Fahrenheit. "
 puts "You're okay."
 temp += 0.1
end while temp < 98.6

puts "Your temperature is " + "%.1f" % temp +
  " Fahrenheit."
```

The output looks like this:

```
Your temperature is 98.3 Fahrenheit. You're okay.
Your temperature is 98.4 Fahrenheit. You're okay.
Your temperature is 98.5 Fahrenheit. You're okay.
Your temperature is 98.6 Fahrenheit. I think you're okay.
Your temperature is 98.7 Fahrenheit.
```

The statement `%.1f" % temp` means format the variable `temp` as a float with one decimal place after the number. See `Kernel#sprintf` for more information on formating strings.

You can break out of a `while` loop with the keyword `break`:

```
while i < breeds.size
 temp << breeds[i].capitalize
 break if temp[i] == "Arabian"
 i +=1
end
p temp # => ["Quarter", "Arabian"]
```

When the `if` modifier following `break` found `Arabian` in the `temp` array, it broke out of the loop immediately.

Statement modifier for while

As with `if`, you can use `while` as a statement modifier at the end of a statement, as shown here:

```
cash = 100_000.00 # underscores are ignored
sum = 0

sum += 1.00 while sum < cash
```

The until Statement

As `unless` is a negated form of `if`, `until` is a negated form of `while`. Compare the following statements:

```
weight = 150
while weight < 200 do
 puts "Weight: " + weight.to_s
 weight += 5
end
```

Here is the same logic expressed with `until`:

```
weight = 150
until weight == 200 do
 puts "Weight: " + weight.to_s
 weight += 5
end
```

And as with `while`, you have another form you can use with `until` and that's with `begin/end`:

```
weight = 150

begin
 puts "Weight: " + weight.to_s
 weight += 5
end until weight == 200
```

In this form, the statements in the loop are evaluated once before the conditional is checked.

Statement modifier for until

And finally, like while, you can also use until as a statement modifier:

```
puts age += 1 until age > 28
```

The case Statement

Ruby's case statement, together with the when clause, provides a way to express conditional logic in a more succinct way. It is similar to the switch statement found in other languages, but case can check objects of any type that can respond to the equality property and/or any equivalence operators, including strings. By the way, case never "falls through" as switch does.

One reason using case/when is more convenient and concise than if/elsif/else is because the logic of == is assumed. Several examples follow. In all case statements, as in the following example (*case.rb*), else is optional:

```
lang = "fr"

dog = case lang
  when "en"
    "dog"
  when "es"
    "perro"
  when "fr"
    "chien"
  when "de"
    "Hund"
  else "dog"
end
```

The string chien is assigned to the variable dog because the value of lang is fr. This example does not print any output.

NOTE

Using a colon (:) instead of a newline or then is deprecated as of 1.9.

If the lang variable held a symbol instead of a string (as in *case_symbol.rb*), the code would look like:

```
lang = :de

doggy = case lang
  when :en then "dog"
  when :es then "perro"
  when :fr then "chien"
  when :de then "Hund"
end
puts doggy
```

The string value Hund is printed to standard output because the value of lang is the symbol :de. The next example (*case_range.rb*) uses several ranges to test the value of a variable (scale). Note the use of semicolons (;) in the when clauses:

```
scale = 8

out = case scale
  when 0 then "lowest"
  when 1..3; "medium-low"
  when 4..5; "medium"
  when 6..7; "medium-high"
  when 8..9; "high"
  when 10; "highest"
  else "off scale"
end
puts "Scale: " + out
```

The result is high because scale is in the range 8 to 9, inclusive. The result is printed to standard output.

This last example (*case_comma.rb*) uses a comma and a Boolean OR operator in the when clause. The comma syntax is considered obscure; using || is recommended:

```
family = "Yukihiro"
given = "Matsumoto"

hi = case
  when family=="Yukihiro", given=="Matsumoto"
    "Hello, Matz!"
  when family == "Thomas" || given == "Dave"
    "Hey, Dave!"
end
puts hi
```

The for Loop

This example of a for loop uses a range (1..10) to print out a list of numbers from 1 to 10, inclusive. The do is optional, unless the for loop is on one line:

```
for i in 1..10 do print i, " " end # => 1 2 3 4 5
  6 7 8 9 10

for i in 1..10
 print i, " "
end # => 1 2 3 4 5 6 7 8 9 10
```

This for loop prints out a single times table (from 1 to 12) for the number 2:

```
for i in 1..12
 print "2 x " + i.to_s + " = ", i * 2, "\n"
end
```

Following is a nested for loop that prints full times tables for multiplicands 1 through 12:

```
for i in 1..12
 for j in 1..12
 print i.to_s + " x " + j.to_s + " = ", j * i, "\n"
 end
end
```

An alternative to the `for` loop, in a similar instance, is the `Integer#times` method:

```
12.times { |i| print i, " " } # => 0 1 2 3 4 5 6 7 8 9 10 11
```

The Conditional Operator

The conditional operator or expression (?:) is a concise structure that descended from C to Ruby. It is also called the *ternary operator* or *base three operator* and is a snug version of `if/then/else`. An example follows:

```
label = length == 1 ? " argument" : " arguments"
```

This expression assigns a string value to `label` based on the value of `length`. If the value of `length` is 1, the string value `argument` (singular) will be assigned to `label`; but if it is not true—that is, `length` has a value other than 1—the string value of `label` will be `arguments` (plural).

Executing Code Before or After a Program

The following structures allow code (*bmi.rb*) to execute *before* and *after* a program runs. Both `BEGIN` and `END` are followed by blocks enclosed by braces ({}):

```
BEGIN { puts "Welcome! Date and time: " + Time.now.to_s }

def bmi( weight, height )
 703.0*( weight.to_f/(height.to_f**2))
end

print "Enter your weight (a number, in lbs.): "
w = gets.chomp.to_f
print "Enter your height (a number, in inches): "
h = gets.chomp.to_f

my_bmi = bmi( w, h )

print "Your BMI is " + x = sprintf( "%0.2f",
  my_bmi ) + " which means you're "

if my_bmi < 18.5 then
  puts "underweight. "
 elsif my_bmi >= 18.5 && my_bmi <= 24.9 then
```

```
  puts "at a healthy weight. "
 elsif my_bmi >= 25.0 && my_bmi <= 29.9 then
  puts "overweight. "
 else
  puts "obese. "
end

END { puts "Try again tomorrow!" }
```

Classes

In an object-oriented programming language like Ruby, a class is a container that holds properties (class members) such as methods and variables. Classes can inherit properties from a parent or superclass, creating a hierarchy of classes with a base class at the root or top. In Ruby, BasicObject is the base, essentially blank class (was Object until 1.9). Ruby uses single inheritance—that is, a Ruby class can inherit the properties of only one parent class. (Multiple inheritance, as in C++, allows a class to inherit from more than one parent.) You can define more than one class in a single file in Ruby. A class itself is an object, even if you don't directly instantiate it. Classes are always open so you can add to any class, even a built-in one.

A class is defined with the keyword class, and the definition concludes with (you guessed it) end:

```
class Hello

 def initialize( name )
  @name = name
 end

 def hello
  puts "Hello, " + @name + "!"
 end

end

hi = Hello.new( "Matz" )
hi.hello # => Hello, Matz!
```

The initialize method defines the instance variable @name by storing a copy of the name argument passed into the initialize method. The `initialize` method is a Ruby convention that acts like a class constructor, but not completely. At this point, the instance is already there, fully instantiated. `initialize` is the first code that is executed *after* the object is instantiated; you can execute just about any Ruby code in `initialize`. `initialize` is always private; that is, it is scoped only to the current object, not beyond it. You can access the instance variable `@name` with the method `hello`.

Reopening a Ruby Class

You can reopen or augment an existing Ruby class. To add a method to an existing Ruby class, for example, such as the built-in class `Array`, you could do something like the following:

```ruby
class Array
  def array_of_ten
    (1..10).to_a
  end
end

arr = Array.new
ten = arr.array_of_ten
p ten # => [1, 2, 3, 4, 5, 6, 7, 8, 9, 10]
```

NOTE

Reopening a built-in class in Ruby might be convenient (it's kind of amazing, really), but there are trade-offs such as the visibility of changes, readability, and so forth. Proceed with caution (but have fun).

Instance Variables

As mentioned previously, an *instance variable* is a variable that is available from within an instance of a class, and is limited in scope because it belongs to a given object. An instance variable is prefixed by a single at sign (@), as in:

```ruby
@name = "Easy Jet"
```

You can define an instance variable inside a method or outside of one, but you can only access an instance variable from outside an object via a method. You can, however, access an instance variable *within* the object without a method:

```
class Horse

  @name = "Easy Jet"

end
```

This works if you only want to reference @name from within the object. You have no way to retrieve the value of @name directly from outside of the object. You must define a getter (accessor) method to retrieve the value:

```
class Horse

  def name
    @name = "Easy Jet"
  end

end

h = Horse.new
h.name # => "Easy Jet"
```

You often want a setter in addition to a getter. A setter is an accessor method that sets the value of a variable:

```
class Horse

  def name
    @name
  end

  def name=( value )
    @name = value
  end

end

h = Horse.new
h.name= "Poco Bueno"
h.name # => "Poco Bueno"
```

The setter method name= follows a Ruby convention: the name of the method ends with an equals sign (=). This convention is not a requirement. You could call name= whatever you like, as long as the characters are legal. Here is another version of the class Horse, which initializes the instance variable @name with the standard initialize method. Later the program creates an instance of the class by calling new, and then accesses the instance variable through the accessor method horse_name, via the instance horse:

```
class Horse

  def initialize( name )
    @name = name
  end

  def horse_name
    @name
  end

end

horse = Horse.new( "Doc Bar" )
puts horse.horse_name # => Doc Bar
```

Accessors

Ruby simplifies the creation of getters and setters by meta-programming with the methods Module#attr, Module#attr_reader, Module#attr_writer, and Module#attr_accessor (Module is the superclass of Class so you can invoke these and other Module methods from any class definition). The attr method creates a single getter method, named by a symbol, with an optional setter method (if the second argument is true):

```
class Dog
 attr :bark, true
end

Dog.instance_methods - Object.instance_methods
  # => [:bark, :bark=]
```

```
dog = Dog.new

dog.bark="Woof!"
puts dog.bark # => Woof!
```

By calling attr with :bark and true as arguments, the class Dog will have the instance methods bark and bark=. If you call attr with only the :bark argument, Dog would have only the getter method bark. (Notice that you can subtract Object's instance methods with - when retrieving Dog's instance methods.)

The attr_reader and attr_writer methods accept as arguments the names of one or more instance variables, and then create corresponding methods that return (attr_reader) or set (attr_writer) the values of each instance variable. (Instance variables are not actually created until you assign values to them.) Consider this example:

```
class Dog
 attr_reader :bark # getter
 attr_writer :bark # setter
end

dog = Dog.new

dog.bark="Woof!"
puts dog.bark # => Woof!

dog.instance_variables.sort # => [:@bark]
Dog.instance_methods.sort - Object.instance_methods
  # => [:bark, :bark=]
```

Calling the attr_accessor method does the same job as calling both attr_reader and attr_writer together, for one or more instance variables:

```
class Gaits
 attr_accessor :walk, :trot, :canter
end

Gaits.instance_methods.sort - Object.instance_methods
  # => [:canter, :canter=, :trot, :trot=, :walk, :walk=]
```

Class Variables

A *class variable* is shared among all instances of a class, so only one copy of a class variable exists for a given class. In Ruby, a class variable is prefixed by two at signs (@@). You *must* initialize a class variable before you use it, such as @@times = 0:

```ruby
class Repeat

@@total = 0

  def initialize( string, times )
    @string = string
    @times = times
  end

  def repeat
    @@total += @times
    return @string * @times
  end

  def total
    "Total times, so far: " + @@total.to_s
  end
end

data = Repeat.new( "ack ", 8 )
ditto = Repeat.new( "Again! ", 5 )
ditty = Repeat.new( "Rinse. Lather. Repeat. ", 2 )

puts data.repeat # => ack ack ack ack ack ack ack ack
puts data.total # => Total times, so far: 8

puts ditto.repeat # => Again! Again! Again! Again!
  Again!
puts ditto.total # => Total times, so far: 13

puts ditty.repeat # => Rinse. Lather. Repeat.
  Rinse. Lather. Repeat.
puts ditty.total # => Total times, so far: 15
```

Class Methods

A *class method* is a method that is associated with a class (and with a module in Ruby), not with an instance of a class. You can invoke class methods by prefixing the name of the method with the name of the class to which it belongs, such as to Math.sqrt(36). Class methods are also called *static methods*. You can also associate the name of a module with a method name, just like with a class, but in order to use such a method, you must include the module in a class. To define a class method, you simply prefix the name of the method with the name of the class or module or the keyword literal self in the method definition. (With Ruby, you can easily add methods to any object. Because classes are objects, adding class methods simply adds methods to the Class object.)

```ruby
class Area

# Use either self.rect or Area.rect
# def self.rect( length, width, units="inches" )
  def Area.rect( length, width, units="inches" )
    area = length * width
    printf( "The area of this rectangle is %.2f %s.",
      area, units )
  end
end

Area.rect(12.5, 16) # => The area of this rectangle is
  200.00 inches.
```

Singletons

Another way to define class methods is by using a class within a class and the keyword literal self. This is called a *singleton* class. A singleton is an object that may be instantiated only once and is often used in place of a global variable. Ruby has a module in its standard library to help create singleton objects; see *http://ruby-doc.org/stdlib-2.2.2/libdoc/singleton/rdoc/Singleton.html*. Singleton takes care of so many things under the hood, such as:

- The new and allocate methods are made private.
- The inherited and clone methods are overridden to ensure that singleton properties are kept when inherited and cloned.

- The `instance` method returns the same object every time it's called.
- The `load` method is overridden to call `instance`.
- The `clone` and `dup` methods are also overridden to raise *TypeErrors* to prevent cloning or duping.

Consider this adaptation that requires the `singleton` library and then includes the `Singleton` module:

```
require 'singleton'

class Area
include Singleton

  def self.rect( length: 10.0, width: 10.0,
                 units: "inches" )
    area = length*width
    printf( "The area of this rectangle is %.2f
            %s.\n", area, units )
  end
end

Area.rect # The area of this rectangle is 100.00 inches.
```

A singleton class is tied to a particular object, can be instantiated only once, and is not distinguished by a prefixed name. The method `Area.rect` is also effectively a *singleton method* because it is tied to the singleton class.

Here is a way to define a singleton method that is tied to a single object:

```
class MySingleton
end

s = MySingleton.new
def s.handle
 puts "I'm a singleton method!"
end

s.handle # => I'm a singleton method!
```

Inheritance

As mentioned earlier, when a child class inherits or derives from a parent, it has access to the methods and properties of the parent class. Inheritance is accomplished with the < operator:

```
class Name
 attr_accessor :given_name, :family_name
end

class Address < Name
 attr_accessor :street, :city, :state, :country
end

a = Address.new
puts a.respond_to?(:given_name) # => true
```

If the class Name were in a different file, you'd just use Kernel#require to load that file first, and then the inheritance operation will work.

Load path

The system path is not necessarily the same thing as the Ruby path or load path. Ruby has a predefined variable called $LOAD_PATH (which also has a Perl-like synonym, $:). $LOAD_PATH is an array that contains the names of directories that are searched by Kernel#load and Kernel#require methods when loading files. Ruby can also use the environment variables PATH and RUBYPATH (if they are set). PATH is the system path and acts as a search path for Ruby programs, among other things; RUBYPATH might be the same thing as PATH, but because it takes precedence over PATH, it is likely to hold other directories beyond it.

Abstract Classes

While Ruby has no special syntax for creating abstract classes or methods, you can still create "abstract" classes and then override (redefine) the method definitions in a concrete class, as shown in the sample program *abstract.rb*. Hello inherits both the hello and bye methods, but because it does not override bye, the call to that method does nothing.

```
class AbstractHello
  def hello;end
  def bye;end
end

class Hello < AbstractHello
  def hello
    puts "Hello"
  end
end

Hello.new.hello
Hello.new.bye
```

Anonymous Classes

If you've coded in other languages, there's no doubt the concept of an *anonymous class* is familiar to you. It is a nameless class that allows you to create class and instance at the same time, which can be useful when you want to be concise (see *http://blog.jayfields.com/2008/02/ruby-creating-anonymous-classes.html*). Here are a few lines of code (*anon.rb*) that illustrate how easy it is to create an anonymous class in Ruby with Class, and then perform some forensics on it. Remember that a class name must be a constant. In this code, the class name is nil until klass is assigned to a constant. Then the magic happens.

```
klass = Class.new #<Class:0x007fae64002340>
klass.name # nil
klass.ancestors # [#<Class:0x007fae64002340>,
  Object, Kernel, BasicObject]
klass.methods # [:allocate, :new, :superclass,
  :freeze, . . .]
MyClass = klass # MyClass
klass.name # "MyClass"
klass.ancestors # [MyClass, Object, Kernel,
  BasicObject]
```

Public, Private, and Protected

The visibility or access of methods and constants might be set with the following methods:

`public`

> The method is accessible by anyone from anywhere; this is the default.

`private`

> The receiver for the method is always the current object or self, so its scope is always the current object (private methods are often helper methods; that is, methods that get called by other methods to perform a task).

`protected`

> The method can be used only by instances of the class where it was defined or by derived classes.

Methods following the keywords `private` or `protected` will have the indicated visibility until changed or until the definition ends (*names.rb*):

```
class Names

  def initialize( given, family, nick, pet )
    @given = given
    @family = family
    @nick = nick
    @pet = pet
  end

  # these methods are public by default

  def given
    @given
  end
```

```
  def family
    @family
  end

# all following methods private, until changed

private

  def nick
    @nick
  end

# all following methods protected, until changed

protected

  def pet
    @pet
  end

end

name = Names.new( "Klyde", "Kimball", "Abner",
  "Teddy Bear" )

name.given # => "Klyde"
name.family # => "Kimball"

# see what happens when you call nick

name.nick # throws a NoMethodError
```

You can also set a method's visibility after its definition, but you must use symbols for method names:

```
protected :pet
```

Modules and Mixins

A Ruby module associates a name with a set of method and constant names. The module name can be used in classes or in other modules by means of the method Module#include. (Note that all classes are modules, as Module is the superclass of Class. This means that you can invoke methods like include from any class.) Generally, the scope or context of such a namespace is the class or module where the namespace (module name) is included.

A module name must be a constant; that is, it must start with an uppercase letter. A module can contain methods, constants, other modules, and even classes. It can inherit from another module, but not from a class. As a class may include a module, it may also include modules that have inherited other modules. Here's an example:

```
module Dice

  # virtual roll of a pair of dice
  def roll
    r_1 = rand(6)
    r_2 = rand(6)
    r1 = r_1>0?r_1:1
    r2 = r_2>0?r_2:6
    total = r1+r2
    printf( "You rolled %d and %d (%d).\n", r1,
      r2, total )
    total
  end

end

class Game
  include Dice
end

g = Game.new
g.roll
```

If the module Dice and the class Game were in separate files, call require 'dice' at the beginning of the file containing the module, before including that module.

When you define module methods like class methods—that is, prefixed with the module name (or with self)—you can call the method as shown here:

```
module Binary

# def self.to_bin( num )
  def Binary.to_bin( num )
    bin = sprintf("%08b", num)
```

```
    end

  end

  Binary.to_bin( 123 ) # => "01111011"
```

Files

You can manipulate file directories (folders) and files from within Ruby programs using methods from the Dir and File classes. For documentation, see *http://www.ruby-doc.org/core-2.2.2/Dir.html* and *http://www.ruby-doc.org/core-2.2.2/File.html*. For example, you can change directories (using an absolute path), and then store the value of the directory path in a variable as follows:

```
Dir.chdir( "/Users/penelope" )
home = Dir.pwd # => "/Users/penelope/"
p home # => "/Users/penelope"
```

If you need a directory, create it with mkdir; later on, delete it with rmdir (or delete, a synonym of rmdir):

```
Dir.mkdir( "/Users/herman/sandbox" )
Dir.rmdir( "/Users/herman/sandbox" )
```

You can also set permissions (the mask 755 sets permissions for owner, group, world [anyone] to rwxr-xr-x where r means *read*, w means *write*, and x means *execute*) on a new directory (not one that already exists) with mkdir:

```
Dir.mkdir( "/Users/floyd/sandbox", 755 )
```

Creating a New File

To create a new file and open it at the same time, use the File method new, like this:

```
file = File.new( "file.rb", "w" )
```

The first argument to new names the new file *file.rb*, and the second argument specifies the file mode: r for readable, w for writable, or x for executable. The effects of the different modes are shown in Table 8.

Table 8. File modes

Mode	Description
"r"	Read-only; starts at beginning of file (default mode).
"r+"	Read-write; starts at beginning of file.
"w"	Write-only; truncates existing file to zero length or creates a new file for writing.
"w+"	Read-write; truncates existing file to zero length or creates a new file for reading and writing.
"a"	Write-only; starts at end of file if file exists, otherwise creates a new file for writing.
"a+"	Read-write; starts at end of file if file exists, otherwise creates a new file for reading and writing.
"b"	(DOS/Windows only) Binary file mode (may appear with any of the key letters listed above).

Opening an Existing File

You can open an existing file with the open method. Use *file*.closed? to test whether a file is closed. It returns true or false:

```
file = File.open( "my_text.txt" )
file.each { |line| print "#{file.lineno}. ", line }
file.closed? # => false
file.close
```

The expression substitution syntax—that is, #{file.lineno}, inserts the line number in the output, followed by the line from the file (see "Expression Substitution" on page 100). The open, each, and close methods are all from the IO class, not File.

ARGV and ARGF

Another interesting way to output the contents of a file is with ARGV, using only two lines of code:

```
ARGV << "my_text.txt"
print while gets
```

ARGV (or $*) is an array, and each of its elements is a filename submitted on the command line, usually. But in this case, we've appended a filename to ARGV directly with <<, which is an array method. You can apply any method to ARGV that you might apply to any other array. For example, try adding this command:

```
p ARGV
```

Or:

```
p ARGV#[0]
```

The Kernel#gets method gets lines from ARGV, and as long as gets returns a string, that line is printed with print.

ARGF ($<) is, once again, a virtual concatenation of all files that appear on the command line:

```
while line = ARGF.gets
 print line
end
```

While there is a line to be retrieved from files on the command line, the code prints that line to standard output. To see how it works, run the program *argf.rb* with several files on the command line:

```
argf.rb my_text.txt my_text_2.txt
```

Both files (if they exist) are printed on the display, one line at a time.

Renaming and Deleting Files

You can rename and delete files programmatically with Ruby using the rename and delete methods. Test these methods by typing these lines into *irb*:

```
File.new( "to_do.txt", "w" )

File.rename( "to_do.txt", "chaps.txt" )

File.delete( "chaps.txt" )
```

File Inquiries

The following command tests whether a file exists before opening it:

```
File.open("file.rb") if File.exists?( "file.rb" )
```

The method exist? (singular) is a synonym of exists?.

Inquire whether the file is really a file by using file?:

```
File.file?( "my_text.txt" ) # => true
```

Or find out if it is a directory by using directory?:

```
# a directory
File.directory?( "/usr/local/bin" ) # => true

# a file
File.directory?( "file.rb" ) # => false
```

Test whether the file is readable by using readable?, writable by using writable?, and executable by using executable?:

```
File.readable?( "mumble.txt" ) # => true
File.writable?( "bumble.txt" ) # => true
File.executable?( "rumble.txt" ) # => false
```

You can find out if a file has a length of zero (0) by using zero?:

```
system("touch blurb.txt") # Create a zero-length
                             file
File.zero?( "blurb.txt" ) # => true

File.size?( "sonnet_129.txt" ) # => 594
File.size( "sonnet_129.txt" ) # => 594
```

The method size is a synonym for size?.

Inquire about the type of a file by using ftype:

```
File.ftype( "file.rb" ) # => "file"
```

The ftype method identifies the type of the file by returning one of the following: file, directory, characterSpecial, blockSpecial, fifo, link, socket, or unknown.

Find out when a file was created, modified, or last accessed by using ctime, mtime, and atime, respectively:

```
File.ctime( "file.rb" ) # => Wed May 08 10:06:37
   -0700 2015
File.mtime( "file.rb" ) # => Wed May 08 10:44:44
   -0700 2015
File.atime( "file.rb" ) # => Wed May 08 10:45:01
   -0700 2015
```

File Modes and Ownership

Use the chmod method with a mask (see Table 9) to change the mode or permissions/access list of a file:

```
file = File.new( "to_do.txt", "w" )
file.chmod( 0755 )
```

Another way to do this:

```
file = File.new( "to_do.txt", "w" ).chmod( 0755 )
system "ls -l" # => -rwxr-xr-x 1 ralphy techw 0 June
   1 22:15 to_do.txt
```

This means that only the owner can write the file, but anyone can read or execute it. Compare it to:

```
file = File.new( "to_do.txt", "w" ).chmod( 0644 )
system "ls -l" # => -rw-r--r-- 1 ralphy techw 0
   May 8 22:13 to_do.txt
```

In this case, everyone can read the file but only the owner can write the file, and no one can execute it.

Table 9. Masks for chmod

Mask	Description
0700	rwx mask for owner
0400	r for owner
0200	w for owner
0100	x for owner
0070	rwx mask for group
0040	r for group

Mask	Description
0020	w for group
0010	x for group
0007	rwx mask for other
0004	r for other
0002	w for other
0001	x for other
4000	Set user ID on execution
2000	Set group ID on execution
1000	Save swapped text, even after use

You can change the owner and group of a file with the chown method, which is like the Unix/Linux command chown (you need superuser or root privileges to use this method):

```
file = File.new( "to_do.txt", "r" )
file.chown( 109, 3333 )
```

Or:

```
file = File.new( "to_do.txt", "r" ).chown( 109,
    3333 )
```

Now perform this system command (works on Unix/Linux systems only) to see the result:

```
system "ls -l to_do.txt"
# => -rw-r--r-- 1 109 3333 0 Nov 8 11:38 to_do.txt
```

The IO Class

The basis for all input and output in Ruby is the IO class, which represents an input/output (I/O) stream of data.

NOTE

Version 2.2.2 has 18 more IO methods than version 1.8.7. This short section can only cover a few of those methods. For more information, see *http://ruby-doc.org/core-2.2.2/IO.html.*

Standard streams include standard input stream ($stdin) or the keyboard; standard output stream ($stdout), which is the display or screen; and standard error output stream ($stderr), which is also the display by default. IO is closely associated with the File class, and File is the only standard subclass of IO in Ruby. Here's a sampling of IO code.

To create a new I/O stream named ios, use the new method. The first argument is 1, which is the *numeric file descriptor* for standard output. Standard output can also be represented by the predefined Ruby variable $stdout (see Table 10). The optional second argument, w, is a mode string meaning *write*:

```
ios = IO.new( 1, "w" )

ios.puts "IO, IO, it's off to work I go ."

$stdout.puts "Do you copy?"
```

Table 10. Standard streams

Stream description	File descriptor	Predefined Ruby global variable	Ruby environment variable
Standard input stream	0	$stdin	STDIN
Standard output stream	1	$stdout	STDOUT
Standard error output stream	2	$stderr	STDERR

Other mode strings include r or read-only (the default), r+ for read-write, and w for write-only. For details on all available modes, see Table 11.

Table 11. I/O modes

Mode	Description
r	Read-only. Starts at the beginning of the file (default mode).
r+	Read-write. Starts at the beginning of the file.
w	Write-only. Truncates existing file to zero length, or creates a new file for writing.
w+	Read-write. Truncates existing file to zero length, or creates a new file for reading and writing.
a	Write-only. Starts at the end of file, if the file exists; otherwise, creates a new file for writing.
a+	Read-write. Starts at the end of the file, if file exists; otherwise, creates a new file for reading and writing.
b	Binary file mode. May appear with any of the modes listed in this table. DOS/Windows only.

With the IO#fileno, test what the numeric file descriptor is for your I/O stream (IO#to_i also works):

```
ios.fileno # => 1
ios.to_i # => 1

$stdout.fileno # => 1
```

You can also write strings to the stream (buffer) with the << method, and then flush the buffer with flush:

```
ios << "Ask not " << "for whom the bell tolls."
    << " -John Donne"

ios.flush # => Ask not for whom the bell tolls.
   -John Donne
```

As of 2.2, when flushing `IO#flush`, don't assume that the metadata of the file is updated immediately. On some platforms (especially Windows), it's delayed until the file system load is decreased. Use `IO#fsync` (not discussed here) if you want to guarantee metadata updates.

Finally, close the stream with `close` (this also flushes any pending writes):

```
ios.close
```

Exception Handling

Exceptions occur when a program has bugs and the normal program flow is interrupted. Ruby is prepared to handle such problems with its own built-in exceptions, but you can handle them in your own way with Ruby's exception handling features. Ruby's model is similar to the C++ and Java models. Table 12 shows a comparison of the keywords or methods used to perform exception handling in the three languages.

Table 12. C++, Java, and Ruby exception handling compared

C++	Java	Ruby
`try {}`	`try {}`	`begin/end`
`catch {}`	`catch {}`	`rescue` keyword (compare with `Kernel#catch` method)
Not applicable	`finally`	`ensure`
`throw`	`throw`	`raise` (compare with `Kernel#throw` method)

I'd like to point out some changes in the `Exception` class since 1.9. For more background information, see *http://www.ruby-doc.org/core-2.2.2/Exception.html*. In 1.9, `to_str` was removed and `==`, which tests if an object is an exception, was added. The `cause` method returns the previous exception (like `$!`), and the array returned by `backtrace_locations` contains different information than the one returned by `backtrace`. Both have been available since 2.1.

The rescue and ensure Clauses

Handle errors/exceptions by using the `rescue` and `ensure` clauses:

```
begin
 eval "1 / 0"
rescue ZeroDivisionError
 puts "Oops. You tried to divide by zero again."
 exit 1
ensure
 puts "Tsk. Tsk."
end
```

The `Kernel#eval` method evaluates a string as a Ruby statement. The result is disastrous, but this time the `rescue` clause catches the error, gives you a custom report in the form of the `Oops` string, and exits the program. (`Kernel#exit`'s argument 1 is a catchall for general errors.) You can have more than one ensure clause if your program calls for it.

Instead of giving its default message—that is, `ZeroDivisionError: divided by 0`—Ruby returns the message in `rescue`, plus the message in `ensure`. Even though the program exited at the end of the `rescue` clause, `ensure` yields its block no matter what.

The raise Method

You don't have to wait for Ruby to raise an exception: you can raise one yourself with `Kernel#raise`. If things go haywire in a program, you can raise an exception, as shown here in *raise.rb*:

```
bad_dog = true

if bad_dog
 raise StandardError, "bad doggy"
else
```

```
  arf_arf
end
```

The program throws the following:

```
raise.rb:4:in '<main>': bad doggy (StandardError)
```

If called without arguments, raise raises a RuntimeError if there was no previous exception. If raise has only a String argument, it raises a RuntimeError with the argument as a message. If the first argument is an exception, such as StandardError, the exception is raised with the given message if such a message is present.

The catch and throw Methods

Kernel#catch executes a block that properly terminates if there is no accompanying Kernel#throw. If a throw accompanies catch, Ruby searches for a catch that has the same symbol as the throw. catch will then return the value given to throw, if present.

NOTE

Calling catch and throw together defines a general-purpose control structure, and though similar, using raise instead of throw is preferred for exception handling.

The following program (*catch.rb*) is an adaptation of an example from Matz's *Ruby in a Nutshell* (O'Reilly, 2002). It defines a method, throw_me, which is called from catch, terminating execution and then exiting. result is then printed to standard output:

```
def throw_me(num)
  throw(:exit, num*num)
end

result = catch(:exit) {
  puts "Before calling throw_me . . ."
```

```
    throw_me(5)
    puts "After calling throw_me" # oops, never executed
}

puts result # returns 25
```

BasicObject Class

The BasicObject class is the Ruby parent class (not Object, as formerly). An explicit blank class, use BasicObject to create object hierarchies that are independent of Ruby's object hierarchy, proxy objects like the Delegator class, or other objects where you want to avoid namespace pollution. BasicObject does not include Kernel and is outside of the namespace of the standard library, so common classes will not be found without using a full class path.

This documentation is adapted and abbreviated from *http://www.ruby-doc.org/core-2.2.2/BasicObject.html*, where you can find code examples and longer explanations. BasicObject's public instance methods are listed next.

BasicObject Public Instance Methods

object!
    Boolean negate.

object! = other
    Returns true if two objects not equal, otherwise false.

object == *other*
    Returns true if objects are same.

object.__id__
    Returns integer identifer for object.

object.__send__(symbol [, args . . .])
    Invokes method identified by symbol, passing any arguments specified.

object.equal? *other*
    Returns true if objects are same. Never override.

```
object.instance_eval(string [, filename [, lineno]] )
```
[or] `object.instance_eval {|obj| block }`
> Evaluates string containing Ruby source code, or block, within context of `object`.

`object.instance_exec(arg . . . ) {|var . . . | block }`
> Executes block within context of `object`.

Object Class

The following public instance methods are part of the `Object` class, which is the former base class of Ruby before `BasicObject` appeared in version 1.9. This documentation is adapted and abbreviated from *http://www.ruby-doc.org/core-2.2.2/Object.html*, where you can find code examples and longer explanations. `Object` includes the `Kernel` module, whose methods are listed in "Kernel Module" on page 82.

To view a list (array) of `Object`'s instance (not singleton) methods, call the `instance_methods` method:

```
Object.instance_methods
```

See also `Module#instance_methods` for details.

Object Public Instance Methods

`object !~ other_object`
> Returns `true` if objects don't match, otherwise `false`.

`object <=> other_object`
> Returns true if objects are same, otherwise `nil`.

`object === other_object`
> Effectively same as == for class `Object`, but typically over-ridden by descendants to provide meaningful semantics.

`object =~ other_object`
> Pattern match. Overridden by descendants to provide meaningful semantics.

object.class
> Returns class of object. Must always have an explicit receiver.

object.clone
> Produces shallow copy of object: copies instance variables, but not objects they reference. Also copies frozen and tainted states of object. Compare Object#dup.

object.dclone
> Provides unified clone operation for REXML.XPathParser to use across multiple object types.

object.define_singleton_method(*symbol, method*) **[or]**
object.define_singleton_method(*symbol*) { *block* }
> Defines singleton method for object; method parameter can be Proc, Method, or UnboundMethod object. If block specified, used as method body.

object.display
> Prints object on given port.

object.dup
> Produces shallow copy of object: copies instance variables, but not objects they reference. Also copies tainted state of object. Compare with Object#clone.

object.enum_for(*method = :each, *args*) **[or]**
object.enum_for(*method = :each, *args*) { |*args| *block* }
> Creates new Enumerator which enumerates by calling method on object, passing args, if any. If block given, it will be used to calculate size of enumerator without need to iterate it.

object == *other_object* **[or]** *object*.equal(*other_object*)
[or] *object*.eql?(*other_object*)
> Returns *true* only if both objects are same; == typically overridden by subclass; should not override equal?; eql? returns true if objects return same hash key.

object.extend(*module*, [...])
>   Adds instance methods from module (one or more) to object.

object.freeze
>   Prevents further modification to object.

object.frozen?
>   Returns frozen status of object.

object.hash
>   Generates Fixnum hash value for object.

object.inspect
>   Returns a human-readable string representation of object.

object.instance_of?(class)
>   Returns true if object is instance of given class.

object.instance_variable_defined?(string) **[or]**
object.instance_variable_defined?(symbol)
>   Returns true if instance variable defined. String arguments converted to symbols.

object.instance_variable_get(string) **[or]**
object.instance_variable_get(symbol)
>   Returns value of instance variable, nil if not set. Include @.

object.instance_variable_set(string) **[or]**
object.instance_variable_set(symbol)
>   Sets instance variable named by symbol to given object, frustrating efforts to provide proper encapsulation. Does not have to exist prior to this call. If instance variable name is passed as a string, that string is converted to symbol.

object.instance_variables
>   Returns array of instance variable names for object.

object.is_a?
> Returns true if object is class of object, or if class is superclass of object or module included in object. Compare Object#kind_of?.

object.itself
> Returns object.

object.kind_of?(class)
> Returns true if object is class of object, or if class is superclass of object or module included in object. Compare with Object#is_a?.

object.method(*symbol*)
> Looks up named method as receiver in object.

object.methods(regular=true)
> Returns list of names of public and protected methods of object.

object.nil?
> Only object nil returns true.

object.__id__ **[or]** *object*.object_id
> Returns integer indentifier for object.

object.private_methods(*all = true*)
> Returns list of private methods accessible to object.

object.protected_methods
> Returns list of protected methods accessible to object.

object.public_method(*symbol*)
> Searches public method symbol in object. Compare with Object#method.

object.public_methods(all=true)
> Returns list of public methods accessible to object. If all = false, only methods in object are listed.

object.public_send(symbol [, args...]) **[or]**
object.public_send(string [, args...])

Invokes method identified by symbol, passing it any specified arguments. Calls public methods only. When method is identified by string, string is converted to symbol.

object.remove_instance_variable(*symbol*)

Removes named instance variable from object, returning that variable's value.

object.respond_to?(*symbol, include_all=false*) **[or]**
object.respond_to?(*string, include_all=false*)

Returns true if object responds to given method. Private and protected methods are included in search only if optional second parameter evaluates to true.

object.respond_to_missing?(*symbol, include_all*) **[or]**
object.respond_to_missing?(*string, include_all*)

Hook method. Returns whether object can respond to ID method or not. Do not use directly.

object.send(symbol [, args...]) **[or]**
object.__send__(symbol [, args...]) **[or]**
object.send(string [, args...]) **[or]**
object.__send__(string [, args...])

Invokes method identified by symbol, passing it any arguments specified. Use __send__ if name send clashes with existing method in object. When method identified by string, it is converted to a symbol.

object.singleton_class

Returns singleton class of object, creating new singleton class if object doesn't have one.

object.singleton_method

Searches for singleton methods only in object. Compare Object#method.

object.singleton_methods(all=true)
> Returns array of names of singleton methods for object. If optional all parameter true, list includes methods in modules included in object. Only public and protected singleton methods are returned.

object.taint
> Mark object as tainted.

object.tainted?
> Returns true if object is tainted.

object.tap { |x|... }
> Yields object to block, then returns block.

object.timeout
> Deprecated. Use Timeout#timeout instead.

object.to_enum(*method* = :each, *args*) **[or]**
object.to_enum(*method* = :each, *args*) {|*args*| *block* }
> Creates new Enumerator, which enumerates by calling method on object, and passing args, if any. If block given, used to calculate size of enumerator without need to iterate it. Compare with Object#Enumerator#size.

object.to_s
> Returns string representation of object.

object.trust
> Deprecated. Compare with Object#untaint.

object.untaint
> Removes tainted mark from *object*.

object.untrust
> Deprecated. Compare with Object#taint.

object.untrusted?
> Deprecated. Compare with Object#tainted?.

`object`.xmp

> Creates new XMP object. Only available when you require
> `IRB.XMP` library.

Kernel Module

These public methods are from the `Kernel` module. (`Kernel` is
included in the `Object` class and other classes.) This documentation is adapted and abbreviated from *http://www.ruby-
doc.org/core-2.2.2/Kernel.html*, where you can find additional
information, code examples, and longer explanations.

`Array(`*argument*`)`

> Returns argument as array.

`BigDecimal(`*argument, [. . .]*`)`

> Returns argument, one or more, as new `BigDecimal` object
> or objects.

`Complex(`*x,y*`)`

> Returns x+i*y as `Complex` object.

`Float(`*argument*`)`

> Returns argument converted to `Float` object.

`Hash(`*argument*`)`

> Converts argument to hash by calling `arg.to_hash`; empty
> when argument is `nil` or `[]`.

`Integer(`*argument*`)`

> Converts argument to `Fixnum` or `Bignum`.

`JSON(`*object, arguments*`)`

> If `object` is string-like, parse string and return parsed
> result as Ruby data structure; otherwise, generate JSON
> text from Ruby data structure object and return it.

`Pathname(`*path*`)`

> Creates new `Pathname` object from path, returns pathname
> object.

Rational(*x*,*y*)
> Returns x/y as Rational object.

String(*argument*)
> Returns argument as string.

URI(*uri_string*)
> Alias for URI.parse.

__callee__
> Returns called name of current method as symbol. If called outside of method, returns nil.

__dir__
> Returns canonicalized absolute path of directory of file from which method is called.

__method__
> Returns name at definition of current method as symbol. If called outside of method, returns nil.

`cmd`
> Returns standard output of running cmd in subshell.

abort **[or]** Kernel#abort(*[message]*) **[or]**
Process.abort(*[message]*)
> Terminate execution immediately, effectively by calling Kernel.exit(false). If message given, written to STDERR prior to terminating.

at_exit { *block* }
> Converts block to Proc object and therefore binds it at point of call, registers it for execution when program exits. If multiple handlers registered, executed in reverse order of registration.

autoload(*module, filename*)
> Registers filename to be loaded first time module accessed.

autoload?(*name*)
> Returns filename to be loaded if name is registered as autoload.

binding

Returns `Binding` object, describing variable and method bindings at point of call.

block_given?

Returns `true` if yield would execute block in current context. Compare `Kernel#iterator?`.

callcc { |*cont*| *block* }

Generates `Continuation` object, which it passes to associated block.

caller(*start = 1, length = nil*) [or] caller(*range*)

Returns current execution stack, which is an array containing strings in form `file:line` or `file:line:` in method. Optional `start` parameter determines number of initial stack entries to omit from top of stack. Second optional `length` parameter limits how many entries returned from stack. Returns `nil` if `start` is greater than size of current execution stack. Optionally, you can pass `range`, which returns array containing entries within specified range.

caller_locations(*start = 1, length = nil*) [or]
caller_locations(*range*)

Returns current execution stack, which is an array containing backtrace location objects. Optional `start` parameter determines number of initial stack entries to omit from top of stack. A second optional `length` parameter limits how many entries are returned from stack. Returns `nil` if `start` is greater than size of current execution stack. Optionally can pass `range`, which returns array containing entries within specified range. Compare with `Thread::Backtrace::Location` for more information.

catch(*[tag]*) { |*tag*| *block* }

Executes its block. If `throw` not called, `block` executes normally and `catch` returns value of last expression evaluated.

chomp **[or]** chomp(*string*)

> Equivalent to $_ = $_.chomp(*string*) where $_ is last line of string, with newline removed. Available only when -p/-n command-line option specified. Compare String#chop.

chop

> Equivalent to ($_.dup).chop! (except nil never returned) where $_ is last line of string, with last character removed. Available only when -p/-n command-line option specified. Compare String#chomp.

eval(*string, binding, filename, lineno*)

> Evaluates Ruby expression(s) in string. If optional binding given, must be Binding object, and evaluation performed in its context. If optional filename and lineno parameters present, used when reporting syntax errors.

exec(*environment*, command . . . , *options*)

> Replaces current process in optional environment by running, given external command with optional options.

exit(*status=true)* **[or]** Kernel.exit(*status = true*) **[or]**
Process.exit(*status = true*)

> Initiates termination of Ruby script by raising SystemExit exception.

exit!(*status = false*)

> Exits process immediately with no exit handlers; status returned to underlying system as exit status.

fail **[or]** fail(*string*) **[or]**
fail(*exception [, string [, array]]*)

> With no arguments, raises exception in $! or raises RuntimeError if $! is nil. With single string argument, raises RuntimeError with string as message. Otherwise, first parameter should be name of Exception class (or object that returns Exception object when sent exception message); optional second parameter string sets message

associated with exception; optional third parameter `array` is array of callback information. Compare `Kernel#raise`.

`Process.fork` **[or]** `Process.fork { ` *block* ` }` **[or]**
`Kernel.fork` **[or]** `Kernel.fork { ` *block* ` }`

Creates subprocess. If block specified, runs in subprocess, and subprocess terminates with status of zero. Otherwise, fork call returns twice: once in parent, returning process ID of child, and once in child, returning `nil`.

`format(`*format_string, arguments,* `. . .)`

Returns string resulting from applying `format_string` to any additional arguments. Within `format_string`, any characters other than format sequences are copied to result. For more information on `format_string`, see `Kernel#sprintf`. Compare `Kernel#printf` and `Kernel#sprintf`.

`gem(`*gem_name, requirements*`)`

Activates specific version of RubyGems `gem_name`; `require` `ments` is list of version requirements that specified gem must match.

`gem_original_require(path)`

The `Kernel#require` from before RubyGems was loaded.

`gets(nil)` **[or]** `gets(`*separator* ` = $/)` **[or]** `gets(`*limit*`)`
[or] `gets(`*separator,limit*`)`

Returns (and assigns to `$_`) next line from list of files in `ARGV` (or `$*`), or from standard input if no files are present on command line. Returns `nil` at end of file. Optional argument specifies record separator and separator is included with contents of each record. `separator` of `nil` reads entire contents, and zero-length `separator` reads input one paragraph at time, where paragraphs are divided by two consecutive newlines. If first argument is integer, or optional second argument `limit` given, returning string would not be longer than given value given in bytes. If multiple filenames are present in `ARGV`, `gets(nil)` reads contents, one file at time.

`global_variables`

Returns array of names of global variables.

`gsub(`*`pattern, replacement`*`)` **[or]** `gsub(`*`pattern`*`) { |...| `*`block`*` }`

Replaces all strings matching `pattern` with `replacement`. Equivalent to `$_.gsub(args)`, except that `$_` will be updated if substitution occurs. Available only when `-p`/`-n` command-line option specified. Compare `Kernel#sub`.

`iterator?`

Returns `true` if yield would execute block in current context; `iterator?` is mildly deprecated. Compare with `Kernel#block_given?`.

`lambda { |...| `*`block`*` }`

Equivalent to `Proc.new`, except resulting `Proc` objects check number of parameters passed when called.

`j(`*`object`*`[, . . .])`

Outputs `object`, zero or more, to `STDOUT` as JSON strings in shortest form—that is, in one line.

`jj(`*`object`*`[, . . .])`

Outputs `object` or objects to `STDOUT` as JSON strings in pretty format, with indentation over many lines.

`load(`*`filename, wrap = false`*`)`

Loads and executes Ruby program in file `filename`. If file name does not resolve to absolute path, file searched for in library directories listed in `$:`. If optional `wrap` parameter is true, loaded script is executed under anonymous module, protecting calling program's global namespace. Local variables in loaded file are propagated to loading environment.

`local_variables`

Returns names of current local variables.

loop **[or]** loop { *block* }

    Repeatedly executes block. If no block given, returns enumerator. StopIteration raised if block breaks loop.

open(path [, mode [, perm]] [, opt]) **[or]**

open(path [, mode [, perm]] [, opt]) {|io| *block* }

    Creates IO object connected to given stream, file, or subprocess. If path does not start with pipe character (|), treat it as name of file to open using specified mode (defaulting to "r"). See IO.new for full documentation of mode string directives.

p **[or]** p(*object*) **[or]** p(*object*[, . . .])

    For each object, one or more, directly write *object*.inspect, followed by newline, to program's standard output. Compare with Kernel#sprintf.

pretty_inspect

    Returns pretty printed object as string. Must require pp.

print(*object*[, . . .])

    Prints each object, one or more, to STDOUT. If output field separator ($,) is not nil, its contents appear between each field. If output record separator ($\) is not nil, it is appended to output. If no arguments given, prints $_. Objects that aren't strings converted by calling their to_s method.

printf(io, *format_string*, *object*[, . . .]) **[or]**

printf(*format_string*, *object*[, . . .])

    Formats object, zero or more, according to format_string. For more information on format_string, see Kernel#sprintf.

proc { |...| *block* }

    Creates new Proc object, bound to current context. Compare with Proc.new.

`putc(int)`

> Prints one character to default output. Compare with IO#putc for information about multibyte characters.

`puts(object[, . . .])`

> Prints object to default output, followed by newline. Compare with Kernel#print.

`raise` **[or]** `raise(string)` **[or]**
`raise(exception [, string [, array]])`

> With no arguments, raises exception in $! or raises RuntimeError if $! is nil. With single string argument, raises RuntimeError with string as message. Otherwise, first parameter should be name of Exception class (or object that returns Exception object when sent exception message). Optional second parameter sets message associated with exception, and third parameter is array of callback information. Exceptions are caught by rescue clause of begin-end blocks.

`rand(max = 0)`

> If called without max argument, or if max.to_i.abs == 0, returns pseudorandom floating-point number between 0.0 and 1.0, including 0.0 and excluding 1.0. When max.abs is greater than or equal to 1, returns pseudo-random integer greater than or equal to 0 and less than max.to_i.abs. When max is range, returns random number where range.member?(number) == true. Negative or floating-point values for max allowed, but results may surprise. Kernel#srand ensures that sequences of random numbers are reproducible between different runs of program. Compare with Kernel#srand and Random#rand.

`readline(separator = $/)` **[or]** `readline(limit)` **[or]**
`readline(separator, limit)`

> Equivalent to Kernel#gets except raises EOFError at end of file. Compare Kernel#gets and Kernel#readlines.

readlines(*separator* = *$/*) **[or]** readlines(*limit*) **[or]**
readlines(*separator, limit*)

> Returns array containing lines returned by calling
> Kernel#gets(*separator*) until end of file. Compare
> Kernel#gets and Kernel#readline.

require(name)

> Loads given name, returning true if successful, false if fea-
> ture already loaded. If filename name does not resolve to
> absolute path, it is searched for in directories listed in
> $LOAD_PATH ($:). If filename name has extension *.rb*, loaded
> as source file; if extension is *.so*, *.o*, or *.dll*, or default
> shared library extension on current platform, Ruby loads
> shared library as Ruby extension. Otherwise, Ruby tries
> adding *.rb*, *.so*, and so on to name until found. If file named
> cannot be found, LoadError is raised.

require_relative(*string*)

> Ruby tries to load library named string, relative to requir-
> ing file's path. If file's path cannot be determined,
> LoadError is raised. If file is loaded, true is returned, false
> otherwise.

scanf(*format, b*)

> Scans STDIN for data matching format. Must require scanf.
> Compare scanf and IO#scanf.

select(*read_array, write_array, error_array, timeout*)

> Calls select(2) system call. Monitors given arrays of IO
> objects, waiting for one or more IO objects until ready for
> reading and writing, and have pending exceptions respec-
> tively, and returns array that contains arrays of those IO
> objects. Returns nil if optional timeout given and no IO
> object is ready in timeout seconds. read_array (required)
> is array of IO objects that waits until ready for read;
> optional write_array is array of IO objects that waits until
> ready for write; optional error_array is array of IO objects
> that waits for exceptions; optional timeout is numeric
> value in seconds.

---

set_trace_func(*proc*) **[or]** set_trace_func(*nil*)

Establishes *proc* as handler for tracing, or disables tracing if parameter is nil. This method is obsolete; please use TracePoint instead.

sleep(duration)

Suspends current thread for optional duration seconds (which may be any number, including Float with fractional seconds). Returns actual number of seconds slept (rounded), which may be less than that asked for if another thread calls Thread#run. If called without argument, sleeps forever.

spawn(*environment, command*[. . .], *options*)

Executes specified command and returns its PID. Similar to Kernel#system but doesn't wait for command to finish. Parent process should use Process.wait to collect termination status of its child or use Process.detach to register disinterest in their status; otherwise, operating system may accumulate zombie processes. Optional environment argument is hash that sets environment variables; required command is command-line string, with possible arguments, passed to shell; optional options is hash (too numerous to list here; see ri Kernel#spawn or online documentation at *ruby-doc.org* from more information). See Kernel#exec for standard shell.

sprintf(*format_string, arguments*[, . . .])

Returns string resulting from applying format_string to any additional arguments. Within format_string, any characters other than format sequences are copied to result. Syntax of format sequence is %[flags][width] [.precision]type. Format sequence consists of percent sign, followed by optional flags, width, and precision indicators, then terminated with field type character. Field type controls how corresponding sprintf argument is to be interpreted, while flags modify that interpretation. Field type characters are listed in Tables 13, 14, and 15.

Table 13. Integer formats

Field	Integer format
b	Convert argument as binary number. Negative numbers will be displayed as two's complement prefixed with ..1.
B	Equivalent to b, but uses uppercase 0B for prefix in alternative format by #.
d	Convert argument as decimal number.
i	Identical to d.
o	Convert argument as octal number. Negative numbers will be displayed as two's complement prefixed with ..7.
u	Identical to d.
x	Convert argument as hexadecimal number. Negative numbers will be displayed as two's complement prefixed with ..f (representing infinite string of leading ffs).
X	Equivalent to x, but uses uppercase letters.

Table 14. Float formats

Field	Float format
e	Convert floating-point argument into exponential notation with one digit before decimal point as [-]d.dddddde[+-]dd. Precision specifies number of digits after decimal point (defaulting to six).
E	Equivalent to e, but uses uppercase E to indicate exponent.
f	Convert floating-point argument as [-]ddd.dddddd, where precision specifies number of digits after decimal point.
g	Convert floating-point number using exponential form if exponent is less than -4 or greater than or equal to precision, or in dd.dddd form otherwise. Precision specifies number of significant digits.
G	Equivalent to g, but use uppercase E in exponent form.
a	Convert floating-point argument as [-]0xh.hhhhp[+-]dd, which consists of optional sign, 0x, fraction part as hexadecimal, p, and exponential part as decimal.

Field	Float format
A	Equivalent to a, but use uppercase X and P.

Table 15. Other formats

Field	Other format
c	Argument is numeric code for single character or single character string itself.
p	The valuing of *argument*.inspect.
s	Argument is string to be substituted. If format sequence contains precision, at most that many characters will be copied.
%	A percent sign itself will be displayed. No argument taken.

The flags modify the behavior of formats. Flag characters are listed in Table 16.

Table 16. Format flags

Flag	Applies to	Meaning
space	bBdiouxX aAeEfgG (numeric format)	Leave space at start of non-negative numbers. For o, x, X, b, and B, use minus sign with absolute value for negative values.
(digit) $	all	Specifies absolute argument number for this field. Absolute and relative argument numbers cannot be mixed in sprintf string.
#	bBoxX aAeEfgG	Use alternative format. For conversions o, increase precision until first digit will be 0 if it is not formatted as complements. For conversions x, X, b, and B on non-zero, prefix result with 0x, 0X, 0b, and 0B, respectively. For a, A, e, E, f, g, and G, force decimal point to be added, even if no digits follow. For g and G, do not remove trailing zeros.

Flag	Applies to	Meaning
+	bBdiouxX aAeEfgG (numeric format)	Add leading plus sign to non-negative numbers. For o, x, X, b, and B, use minus sign with absolute value for negative values.
-	all	Left-justify result of this conversion.
0 (zero)	bBdiouxX aAeEfgG (numeric format)	Pad with zeros, not spaces. For o, x, X, b, and B, radix-1 is used for negative numbers formatted as complements.
*	all	Use next argument as field width. If negative, left-justify result. If asterisk is followed by number and dollar sign ($), use indicated argument as width.

srand(*number = Random.new_seed*)

Seeds system pseudo-random number generator, Random::DEFAULT, with number. Previous seed value is returned. If number is omitted, seeds generator using source of entropy provided by operating system, if available (/dev/urandom on Unix systems or RSA cryptographic provider on Windows), which is then combined with time, process id (PID), and sequence number. May be used to ensure repeatable sequences of pseudorandom numbers between different runs of program. By setting seed to known value, programs can be made deterministic during testing.

sub(*pattern, replacement*) **[or]**
sub(*pattern*) { |...| *block* }

Replaces all strings matching pattern with replacement. Equivalent to $_.sub(args), except that $_ will be updated if substitution occurs. Available only when -p/-n command-line option specified. Compare Kernel#gsub.

syscall(*number, arguments[, . . .]*)

Calls operating system function identified by number and returns result of function or raises SystemCallError if failed. Optional `arguments` for function may follow `number`. They must be either `String` or `Integer` objects. `String` object passed as pointer to byte sequence; `Integer` object passed as integer whose bit size is same as pointer. Up to nine parameters may be passed (14 on Atari-ST). `syscall` is essentially unsafe and unportable. DL (Fiddle) library is preferred for safer and more portable programming.

`system(environment, command . . ., options)`

Executes `command` in subshell, in one of following forms:

`commandline`

Command-line string that is passed to standard shell.

`cmdname, arg1, . . .`

Command name and one or more arguments (no shell).

`cmdname, argv0, arg1, . . .`

Command name, `argv[0]`, and zero or more arguments (no shell).

Returns `true` if command gives zero exit status, `false` for non-zero exit status, `nil` if command execution fails. An error status is available in `$?`. Arguments are processed in same way as for `Kernel#spawn`. Compare `Kernel#exec` for standard shell.

`test(command, file1, file2)`

Uses `command` (a character) to perform various tests on `file1` or on `file1` and `file2`. Table 17 lists tests on single files.

Table 17. File tests

Command	Returns	Meaning
A	Time	Last access time for `file1`
b	Boolean	True if `file1` is block device
c	Boolean	True if `file1` is character device
C	Time	Last change time for `file1`

Command	Returns	Meaning
d	Boolean	True if file1 exists and is directory
e	Boolean	True if file1 exists
f	Boolean	True if file1 exists and is regular file
g	Boolean	True if file1 has \CF{setgid} bit set (false under NT)
G	Boolean	True if file1 exists and has group ownership equal to caller's group
k	Boolean	True if file1 exists and has sticky bit set
l	Boolean	True if file1 exists and is symbolic link
M	Time	Last modification time for file1
o	Boolean	True if file1 exists and is owned by caller's effective uid
O	Boolean	True if file1 exists and is owned by caller's real uid
p	Boolean	True if file1 exists and is FIFO
r	Boolean	True if file1 is readable by effective UID/GID of caller
R	Boolean	True if file1 is readable by real UID/GID of caller
s	int/nil	If file1 has nonzero size, return size; otherwise, return nil
S	Boolean	True if file1 exists and is socket
u	Boolean	True if file1 has setuid bit set
w	Boolean	True if file1 exists and is writable by effective UID/GID
W	Boolean	True if file1 exists and is writable by real UID/GID
x	Boolean	True if file1 exists and is executable by effective UID/GID

Command	Returns	Meaning
x	Boolean	True if file1 exists and is executable by real UID/GID
z	Boolean	True if file1 exists and has zero length

Tests in Table 18 take two files.

Table 18. File tests for two files

-	Boolean	True if file1 and file2 are identical
=	Boolean	True if modification times of file1 and file2 are equal
<	Boolean	True if modification time of file1 is prior to that of file2
>	Boolean	True if modification time of file1 is after that of file2

throw(tag, object)

Transfers control to end of active catch block waiting for tag. Raises UncaughtThrowError if there is no catch block for tag. Optional second parameter object supplies return value for catch block, which otherwise defaults to nil. Compare Kernel#catch.

trace_var(*symbol, command*) **[or]**
trace_var(symbol) { |val| block }

Controls tracing of assignments to global variables. Parameter symbol identifies variable (as either string name or symbol identifier); command (which may be string or Proc object) or block is executed whenever variable is assigned. Block or Proc object receives variable's new value as parameter. Compare Kernel#untrace_var.

trap(*signal, command*) **[or]** trap(*signal*) { |...| *block* }

Specifies handling of signals. First parameter, signal, is signal name (a string such as SIGALRM, SIGUSR1, and so on) or signal number. Characters SIG may be omitted from signal names; command or block specifies code to be run when signal is raised. If command is string IGNORE or SIG_IGN, signal is ignored. If command is DEFAULT or

SIG_DFL, Ruby's default handler is invoked. If command is EXIT, script is terminated by signal. If command is SYSTEM_DEFAULT, operating system's default handler is invoked. Otherwise, given command or block runs. Special signal name EXIT or signal number zero (0) is invoked just prior to program termination. Returns previous handler for given signal.

untrace_var(*symbol,* command)
Removes tracing for specified command on given global variable and returns nil. If no command specified, removes all tracing for that variable and returns array containing commands actually removed.

warn(*message [, . . .]*)
Displays each given message, followed by record separator on STDERR, unless warnings have been disabled (for example, with -W0 flag).

String Class

A String object in Ruby holds an arbitrary sequence of one or more characters written in human language. Ruby has a built-in class called String that defines a number of methods used frequently when programming Ruby. Those methods are listed and described briefly in this section. Following are some string-related features of Ruby.

String Literals

In most cases, the value of a string literal in Ruby is enclosed in either single or double quotes. Single-quoted strings have the following characteristics:

- Are enclosed in or surrounded by single quotes or apostrophe characters (')
- Allow backslash notation only for a literal single quote or apostrophe (\') and a literal backslash character (\\)

- Can extend over multiple lines when a backslash character (\) appears at the end of a line
- Must escape newlines with '\ to avoid embedding newlines in the string
- Don't allow expression substitution

Following is an example of a single-quoted string:

```
'This isn\'t such a bad day and  '\
'and that\'s the truth.'
```

Double-quoted strings have the following traits:

- Are enclosed in or surrounded by double-quote characters (")
- Allow backslash notation (\n [newline], \t [tab], and so forth)
- Allow the entry of Unicode characters (in UTF-8 encoding) in the form \u*xxxx* in the range 0000 and FFFF (cannot drop leading zeros), or \u{*xxxxxx*} in the range 0 and 10FFFF (can drop leading zeros), or multiple codepoints in the form \u{*xxxxxx[xxxxxx . . .]*} (one to six hexadecimal digits, separated by spaces or tabs)
- Allow the entry of octal digits in the form \o*nnn* (one to three digits in the ranges 0 to 7, 00 to 77, and 000 and 377, respectively)
- Allow non-terminating quote marks when escaped with a backslash, as in \"
- Can extend multiple lines with a backslash character (\) at the end of a line
- Allow expression substitution (string interpolation) with #{*expr*}. Here is a double-quoted string:

```
"This isn't a single-quoted string\n\
and it works just grand, don't it?"
```

See also "Here Documents" on page 101.

String Concatenation

You can concatenate or join strings in Ruby in several ways—
with or without a plus sign. The following two concatenations
produce the same result:

```
str1 = "Hello, " "world!"
str2 = "Hello, " + "world!"
str1 == str2 # true
puts str1
puts str2
```

NOTE

The method String#concat is a synonym for an append
operation (<<), not a concatenation.

Expression Substitution

Expression substitution is a means of embedding the value of
any Ruby expression into a string using #{ and }, as shown here
(*string_interp.rb*):

```
x, y, z = 12, 36, 72

puts "The value of x is #{ x }."

puts "The sum of x and y is #{ x + y }."

puts "The average was #{ (x + y + z)/3 }."
```

The output of this program is:

```
The value of x is 12.
The sum of x and y is 48.
The average was 40.
```

You can embed global variables and instance variables in
abbreviated form, like this:

```
$glob = "global variable"
puts "This syntax works for a #$glob." # same as
  #{$glob}
```

```
@inst = "instance variable"
puts "This syntax works for an #@inst." # same as
  #{@inst}
```

Expression substitution is also called *string interpolation*. You can also perform string interpolation with Kernel#printf, IO#printf, and Kernel#sprintf. See Kernel#sprintf for more information.

General Delimited Strings

With *general delimited strings*, you can create strings inside of a pair of matching, arbitrary delimiter characters; for example, !, (, {, <, etc., preceded by a percent character (%). Q, q, and x have special meanings. Escape with backslash (\). General delimited strings can be nested. Here are a few examples:

```
%|Ecclesiastes| # follows double-quoted string rules

%Q{ Hamlet } # follows double-quoted string rules

%q[Much Ado about Nothing] # follows single-quoted
   string rules

%r!Middlemarch! # regular expression pattern,
   equivalent to /Middlemarch/

%x!ls! # => equivalent to backticked (`) command
   output for ls
# => "file.ext\nanother_file.ext\nyet_another_file.ext\n"
```

Here Documents

A *here document* (or sometimes *heredoc*) is a useful bit of syntax borrowed from Unix that allows you to quickly build multi-line strings inside a nested pair of identifiers, preceded by << or <<-. The characters that follow have special meaning:

<<

Delimiter followed by no intervening space, then optionally by a single- or double-quote, then by an identifier (string) that, if quoted, may or may not contain whitespace. This identifier is also used at the end of the document that appears on a line by itself following the string literal (the here document itself). If present earlier, paired with a single- or double-quote, following the identifier. May be followed by a comment.

`<<-`

Same as << but closing identifier may be indented or preceded with whitespace.

`'`

Optional. Precedes and follows identifier, which may in this case contain whitespace. No need to escape the single quote (apostrophe) or backslash; they are interpreted literally. Must be paired with another single quote.

`"`

Same as single quote.

`` ` ``

2153.140If the identifier is enclosed in backticks, the string literal will be interpreted as a system command.

`#`

Precedes a comment but only on the first line. It's never part of the string literal.

Here are several examples:

```
puts <<x # double-quoted string
To every thing there is a season,
and a time to every purpose
under the heaven.
x

# double-quoted string, assigned to variable hamlet
hamlet = <<"poor yorick"
Alas, poor Yorick! I knew him, Horatio: a fellow
of infinite jest, of most excellent fancy: he hath
borne me on his back a thousand times; and now, how
abhorred in my imagination it is! my gorge rims at
it. Here hung those lips that I have kissed I know
not how oft.
poor yorick

# single-quoted string
puts <<'Benedick'
Shall quips and sentences and these paper bullets
```

```
of the brain awe a man from the career of his
humour? No, the world must be peopled. When I
said I would die a bachelor, I did not think I
should live till I were married. Here comes
Beatrice. By this day! she's a fair lady: I do
spy some marks of love in her.
Benedick

# back-quoted string
dir = <<`listdir`
ls -l
listdir

# indented string
puts <<-cummings
 it's
 spring
 and
 the

 goat-footed

 balloonMan whistles
 far
 and
 wee
 cummings
```

Escape Characters

Table 19 provides a list of escape or non-printable characters
that can be represented with backslash notation. In a double-
quoted string, an escape character is interpreted; in a single-
quoted string, an escape character is preserved.

Table 19. Escape (non-printable) characters

Notation	Hexadecimal value	Description
\x		Backslash before any character is same as character by itself, except special characters in this table
\a	0x07	BEL or bell (ASCII decimal 7)

Notation	Hexadecimal value	Description
\b	0x08	BS or backspace (ASCII decimal 8)
\cx		Shorthand for \C-x
\C-x		Though x can be any character, it is usually control sequence where x is in range A–Z (ASCII decimal 1–26) but can use upper- or lowercase
\e	0x1b	ESC or escape (ASCII decimal 27)
\eol		Escapes line terminator
\f	0x0c	FF or formfeed (ASCII decimal 12)
\M-x		Metacharacter sequence where x typically > 126
\n	0x0a	LF or newline (ASCII decimal 10)
\n		Octal notation in range 0–7
\nn		Octal notation in range 00–77
\nnn		Octal notation in range 000–377
\r	0x0d	CR or carriage return (ASCII decimal 13)
\s	0x20	SP or space (ASCII decimal 32)
\t	0x09	TAB (ASCII decimal 9)
\unnnn		Unicode codepoint. Each n is a hexadecimal digit. May not drop leading zeros (since Ruby 1.9).
\u{hex digits}		Unicode codepoint in range 0–10FFFF. May drop leading zeros (since Ruby 1.9).
\v	0x0b	VT or vertical tab (ASCII decimal 11)
\xn		Hexadecimal notation in range 0–F (upper- and lowercase allowed)
\xnn		Hexadecimal notation in range 00–FF (upper- and lowercase allowed)

Character Encoding

Ruby now offers robust encoding support. Since version 1.9, Ruby strings have been composed of sequences of characters instead of bytes or integers as in previous versions. Before version 1.9, a string in Ruby was a sequence of bytes, or numbers representing characters. The `String` class was rewritten to accommodate this change. A character is now represented as a string of length 1. See *http://ruby-doc.org/core-2.2.2/Encoding.html*.

When would you use encoding? If, for example, you wanted to use the Japanese Hiragana script in Ruby, you could set your encoding to `EUC_JP` or `Shift_JIS`.

The `-K` command-line option has been replaced by the `-E` and `--encoding` command-line options; and instead of the `$KCODE` global variable, you can now use the `__ENCODING__` keyword to obtain the source encoding, returned as an `Encoding` object. This keyword is both preceded and followed by a pair of underscores (`_`). Here's several ways you can use the new command-line option:

```
ruby -E US-ASCII hello.rb
ruby --encoding=UTF-8 myprog.rb
```

You can also set the encoding with a magic or coding comment appearing on the first line of a program, or if the program uses a shebang comment, as a second line. An example coding comment is shown here:

```
# coding: EUC_JP
```

Table 20 shows several common encoding values for Ruby as a sample. Calling the class method `Encoding.name_list` returns an array containing available encoding values or names—170 of them in version 2.2.

Table 20. Common encoding values

Encoding	Description
ASCII-8BIT	8-bit ASCII (same as BINARY)

Encoding	Description
BINARY	Alias for 8-bit ASCII (same as ASCII-8BIT)
EUC-JP	EUC-JP (Japanese)
ISO-8859-1 – ISO-8859-16	ISO/IEC 8859 8-bit, single-byte coded graphic character sets
SHIFT_JIS	SHIFT_JIS (Japanese)
SJIS	Alias for SHIFT_JIS (Japanese)
US-ASCII	7-bit ASCII
UTF-8	Multibyte UTF-8
UTF-16	Multibyte UTF-16
UTF-32	Multibyte UTF-32

Regular Expressions

A regular expression is a special sequence or pattern of characters that helps you match or find other strings or sets of strings using a specialized syntax. See *http://ruby-doc.org/core-2.2.2/Regexp.html*. Ruby is supported by the Oniguruma regular expression library (see *http://www.geocities.jp/kosako3/oniguruma/*).

Strings are matched with regular expression patterns, delimited with a pair of slashes (/) or r%{ }. Here is a string (opening) that contains the first two lines of Shakespeare's Sonnet 29. The match operator =~ finds the pattern /beweep/ starting at character position 57:

```
opening = "When in disgrace with fortune and men's
  eyes\nI all alone beweep my outcast state,\n"
/beweep/ =~ opening
=> 57
```

The !˜ operator returns true when a pattern *does not* match a string; it is false otherwise:

```
%r{wept} !~ opening
=> true
```

```
%r{beweep} !~ opening
=> false
```

The method `Regexp#match` returns a matched pattern, `nil` otherwise:

```
mat = opening.match(/beweep/)
=> #<MatchData "beweep">
```

The `MatchData` class encapsulates the results of a matched pattern, and those results can be accessed by predefined globals and methods such as `$~` (the `MatchData` object), `$&` (the last match [`Regexp.last_match`]), `$`` (or `Regexp#pre_match`), and `$'` (or `Regexp#post_match`). See Table 30 and *http://www.ruby-doc.org/core-2.2.2/MatchData.html*.

Let's take a moment to look at what is now in the `MatchData` object `mat` using some predefined global variables and a few methods from this class (*match.rb*):

```
opening = "When in disgrace with fortune and men's
  eyes\nI all alone beweep my outcast state,\n"
mat = opening.match(/beweep/)
p $~ # <MatchData "beweep">
p $& == Regexp.last_match.to_s # true
p mat == Regexp.last_match # true
p $& # "beweep"
p mat.to_s # "beweep"
p $` # "When in disgrace with fortune and men's
  eyes\nI all alone "
p mat.pre_match # "When in disgrace with fortune and men's
  eyes\nI all alone "
p $' # " my outcast state,\n"
p mat.post_match # " my outcast state,\n"
```

`MatchData` has 19 methods, most of which are not mentioned here.

Alternation lets you match alternate forms of a pattern using the bar (`|`):

```
opening.match(/men|man/)
=> #<MatchData "men">
```

Grouping uses parentheses to group a subexpression, like this one that contains an alternation:

```
opening.match /m(e|a)n/
=> #<MatchData "men" 1:"e">
```

Anchors anchor a pattern, such as to the beginning of a line with a caret (^) or the end of a line with a dollar sign ($), like so:

```
opening.match /^When in/
=> #<MatchData "When in">
opening.match /outcast state,$/
=> #<MatchData "outcast state,">
```

See Table 22 for a list of available anchors.

Character shorthands are single characters preceded by a backslash that have special meaning. For example, the \d shorthand represents a digit; it is the same as using character class [0-9]. Similarly to ^, the shorthand \A matches the beginning of a string, not a line. The shorthand \z matches the end of a string, not a line, similarly to $. The shorthand \Z matches the end of a string before the newline character, assuming that a newline character (\n) is at the end of the string (it won't work otherwise).

To match a three-digit number in the form 123, try this:

```
str = "Easy as 123"
str.match /\d\d\d/
=> #<MatchData "123">
```

Or try:

```
str.match /\d+/
```

The plus sign (+) is a *repetition operator*. It means one or more occurrences of the previous pattern. Another repetition operator is ?, which means zero or one occurrence. Here is a way to use ? with just a single character, *u*:

```
color_us = "color"
colour_uk = "colour"
color_us.match /colou?r/
=> #<MatchData "color">
colour_uk.match /colou?r/
=> #<MatchData "colour">
```

An asterisk (*) operator indicates zero or more occurrences. Braces ({}) let you specify the exact number of digits, like \d{3} or \d{4}:

```
phone = "555-123-4567"
phone.match /\d{3}-\d{3}-\d{4}/
```

It is also possible to indicate an *at least* amount with {m,}, and a minimum/maximum amount with {m,n}.

Regular Expression Reference Tables

Character classes. Table 21 shows examples of character classes. A hyphen (-) denotes a range, as in [0-1]. A caret (^) has the effect of negation and does not mean "at the beginning of the line." You must escape square brackets and hyphens if you want them to be interpreted literally (\[, \], and \-). You can also use && lower precedence in a character class, as in [a-w&&[^c-g]z] ==& ([a-w] AND ([^c-g] OR z)) ==> [abh-w] (See *http://www.geocities.jp/kosako3/oniguruma/doc/RE.txt*).

Table 21. Character classes in Ruby regular expressions

Character Class	Description
[.]	Matches any character except a newline (unless in multiline mode)
[a-zA-Z0-9_]	Matches word characters (compare with \w)
[^a-zA-Z0-9_]	Matches non-word characters (compare with \W)
[0-9]	Matches digits (compare with \d)
[^0-9]	Matches non-digits (compare with \D)
[0-9a-fA-F]	Matches hexdigits (compare with \h)
[^0-9a-fA-F]	Matches non-hexdigits (compare with \H)
[\t\r\n\f]	Matches whitespace characters (compare with \s)
[^ \t\r\n\f]	Matches non-whitespace characters (compare with \S)

Anchors. Table 22 lists Ruby's anchor metacharacters.

Table 22. Anchor metacharacters in Ruby regular expressions

Metacharacter(s)	Description
^	Matches beginning of line
$	Matches end of line
\A	Matches beginning of string
\b	Matches word boundaries when outside brackets; backspace (0x08) when inside brackets
\B	Matches non-word boundaries
\G	Matches point where last match finished or start position
\z	Matches end of string
\Z	Matches end of string. If string ends with a newline, it matches just before newline.

Character shorthands. Table 23 shows character shorthands (also known as *character class metacharacters*).

Table 23. Character shorthands in Ruby regular expressions

Shorthand	Description
.	Matches any character except a newline (unless in multiline mode)
\a	Matches bell character
[\b]	Matches backspace character (must be used in a character class)
\cx	Matches control character
\C-x	Matches control character
\d	Matches decimal digit character ([0-9])
\D	Matches non-digit character ([^0-9])
\e	Matches escape character

Shorthand	Description
\f	Matches formfeed character
\h	Matches hexdigit character ([0-9a-fA-F])
\H	Matches non-hexdigit character ([^0-9a-fA-F])
\M-x	Matches metacharacter
\M-\Cx	Matches meta-control character
\n	Newline
\nnn	Octal character
\r	Return
\s	Matches whitespace character ([\t\r\n\f])
\S	Matches non-whitespace character ([^ \t\r\n\f])
\t	Tab
\v	Vertical tab
\w	Matches word character ([a-zA-Z0-9_])
\W	Matches non-word character ([^a-zA-Z0-9_])
\xhh	Hexadecimal character
\x{hhhhhhhh}	Hexadecimal character (wide)

POSIX bracket expressions. POSIX bracket expressions are similar to character classes and are a portable alternative to them, but also match non-ASCII characters. /\d/ only matches ASCII decimal digits 0 through 9 but /[[:digit:]]/ matches any character in the Unicode *Nd* category. These can be negated, as in [[:^blank:]]. Table 24 lists POSIX expressions.

Table 24. POSIX bracket expressions in Ruby regular expressions

Expression	Description
[[:alnum:]]	Alphabetic and numeric character
[[:alpha:]]	Alphabetic character

Expression	Description
`[[:ascii:]]`	A character in the ASCII character set (non-POSIX)
`[[:blank:]]`	Space or tab
`[[:cntrl:]]`	Control character
`[[:digit:]]`	Digit
`[[:graph:]]`	Non-blank character (excludes spaces, control characters, and similar)
`[[:lower:]]`	Lowercase alphabetical character
`[[:print:]]`	Like `[:graph:]`, but includes the space character
`[[:punct:]]`	Punctuation character
`[[:space:]]`	Whitespace character (`[:blank:]`, newline, carriage return, etc.)
`[[:upper:]]`	Uppercase alphabetical
`[[:word:]]`	A character in one of the following Unicode general categories *Letter, Mark, Number, Connector_Punctuation* (non-POSIX)
`[[:xdigit:]]`	Digits allowed in hexadecimal number (0-9a-fA-F)

Quantifiers. Quantifiers (also called *repetition operators* or *repetition metacharacters*) are shown in Table 25. A *greedy* match attempts to match the whole target string and then backtracks one character at a time. A *reluctant* or lazy match looks at the target one character at a time. A *possessive* match is greedy but does not backtrack.

Table 25. Quantifiers in Ruby regular expressions

Quantifier	Description
`*`	Zero or more times (greedy)
`+`	One or more times (greedy)
`?`	Zero or one times (optional) (greedy)

Quantifier	Description
{n}	Exactly n times (greedy)
{n,}	n or more times (greedy)
{,m}	m or less times (greedy)
{n,m}	At least n and at most m times (greedy)
*?	Zero or more times (reluctant or lazy)
+?	One or more times (reluctant)
??	Zero or one times (optional) (reluctant or lazy)
{n}?	Exactly n times (reluctant or lazy)
{n,}?	n or more times (reluctant or lazy)
{,m}?	m or less times (reluctant or lazy)
{n,m}?	At least n and at most m times (reluctant or lazy)
*+	Zero or more times (possessive)
++	One or more times (possessive)
?+	Zero or one times (optional) (possessive)

Character properties. The \p{} construct matches characters with a named property, similar to the POSIX bracket classes. Table 26 lists these properties. You can negate these with \p{^property} or \P{property}.

Table 26. Character properties in Ruby regular expressions

Property	Description
\p{Any}	Any Unicode character (including unassigned characters)
\p{ASCII}	A character in the ASCII character set
\p{Assigned}	An assigned character
\p{Alnum}	Alphabetic and numeric character
\p{Alpha}	Alphabetic character
\p{Blank}	Space or tab

Property	Description
\p{Cntrl}	Control character
\p{Digit}	Digit
\p{Graph}	Non-blank character (excludes spaces, control characters, and similar)
\p{Hiragana}	Hiragana script with encodings EUC_JP or Shift_JIS
\p{Katakana}	Katakana script with encodings EUC_JP or Shift_JIS
\p{Lower}	Lowercase alphabetical character
\p{Print}	Like \p{Graph}, but includes the space character
\p{Punct}	Punctuation character
\p{Space}	Whitespace character ([:blank:], newline, carriage return, etc.)
\p{Upper}	Uppercase alphabetical
\p{XDigit}	Digits and characters allowed in a hexadecimal number (0-9a-fA-F)
\p{Word}	A member of one of the following Unicode general category Letter, Mark, Number, Connector_Punctuation

Unicode character categories. Table 27 lists abbreviations for general Unicode character categories. You can negate these with \p{^property} or \P{property}. These work with UTF8, UTF16, and UTF32.

Table 27. General categories for Ruby regular expressions

Category	Description
\p{C}	'Other'
\p{Cc}	'Other: Control'
\p{Cf}	'Other: Format'
\p{Cn}	'Other: Not Assigned'
\p{Co}	'Other: Private Use'

Category	Description
\p{Cs}	'Other: Surrogate'
\p{L}	'Letter'
\p{Ll}	'Letter: Lowercase'
\p{Lm}	'Letter: Mark'
\p{Lo}	'Letter: Other'
\p{Lt}	'Letter: Titlecase'
\p{Lu}	'Letter: Uppercase
\p{M}	'Mark'
\p{Mc}	'Mark: Spacing Combining'
\p{Me}	'Mark: Enclosing'
\p{Mn}	'Mark: Nonspacing'
\p{N}	'Number'
\p{Nd}	'Number: Decimal Digit'
\p{Nl}	'Number: Letter'
\p{No}	'Number: Other'
\p{P}	'Punctuation'
\p{Pc}	'Punctuation: Connector'
\p{Pd}	'Punctuation: Dash'
\p{Pe}	'Punctuation: Close'
\p{Pf}	'Punctuation: Final Quote'
\p{Pi}	'Punctuation: Initial Quote'
\p{Po}	'Punctuation: Other'
\p{Ps}	'Punctuation: Open'
\p{S}	'Symbol'
\p{Sc}	'Symbol: Currency'
\p{Sk}	'Symbol: Modifier'

Category	Description
\p{Sm}	'Symbol: Math'
\p{So}	'Symbol: Other'
\p{Z}	'Separator'
\p{Zl}	'Separator: Line'
\p{Zp}	'Separator: Paragraph'
\p{Zs}	'Separator: Space'

Unicode scripts.   Table 28 shows the Unicode language scripts that Ruby supports.

Table 28. Unicode scripts for Ruby regular expressions

Script	Script	Script
Arabic	Hac	Oriyc
Armeniac	Hanguc	Osmanyc
Balinesc	Hanunoc	Phags_Pc
Bengalc	Hebrec	Phoeniciac
Bopomofc	Hiraganc	Rejanc
Braillc	Inherited	Runic
Buginesc	Kannadc	Saurashtrc
Buhic	Katakanc	Shaviac
Canadian_Aboriginac	Kayah_LcKharoshthc	Sinhalc
Cariac	Khmec	Sundanesc
Chac	Lac	Syloti_Nagrc
Cherokec	Latin	Syriac
Commoc	Lepchc	Tagaloc
Coptic	Limbc	Tagbanwc
Cuneiforc	Linear_c	Tai_Lc

Script	Script	Script
Cyprioc	Lyciac	Tamic
Cyrillic	Lydiac	Telugc
Deserec	Malayalac	Thaanc
Devanagarc	Mongoliac	Thac
Ethiopic	Myanmac	Tibetac
Georgiac	New_Tai_Luc	Tifinagc
Glagolitic	Nkc	Ugaritic
Gothic	Oghac	Vac
Greec	Ol_Chikc	Yi
Gujaratc	Old_Italic	
Gurmukhc	Old_Persiac	

Modifiers (options). Table 29 lists the four modifiers or options you can used with patterns.

Table 29. Modifiers (options) in Ruby regular expressions

Modifier	Description
/*pattern*/i	Ignore case (or constant Regexp::IGNORECASE)
/*pattern*/m	Treat a newline as a character matched by a full stop or period (.) (or constant Regexp::MULTILINE)
/*pattern*/x	Ignore whitespace and comments in the pattern (or constant Regexp::EXTENDED)
/*pattern*/o	Perform #{} interpolation only once

Special global variables. Several global variables are available that have special meaning with regard to regular expressions, as shown in Table 30.

Table 30. Special global variables in Ruby regular expressions

Global Variable	Description
$~	Equivalent to ::last_match
$&	Contains the complete matched text
$`	Contains string before match
$'	Contains string after match
$1, $2, etc.	Contains text matching first, second, etc. capture group
$+	Contains last capture group

Encoding overrides. You can override the source character encoding with one of the four options shown in Table 31.

Table 31. Encoding for Ruby regular expressions

Option	Description
/*pattern*/u	UTF-8
/*pattern*/e	EUC-JP
/*pattern*/s	Windows-31J
/*pattern*/n	ASCII-8BIT

Extended groups. Table 32 shows extended groups, including lookaheads and lookbehinds.

Table 32. Extended groups in Ruby regular expressions

Group	Description
(?# . . .)	Comment
(?i) **[or]** (?-i)	Ignore case (on/off)
(?m) **[or]** (?-m)	Multiline mode (on/off)
(?x) **[or]** (?-x)	Extended form (on/off)
(?[i|m|x]-[i|m|x]:*subexp*)	Options (on/off) for subexp

Group	Description
(?:*subexp*)	Non-captured group
(*subexp*)	Captured group
(?=*pattern*)	Positive lookahead assertion: ensures that the following characters match pattern, but doesn't include those characters in the matched text
(?!*pattern*)	Negative lookahead assertion: ensures that the following characters do not match pattern, but doesn't include those characters in the matched text
(?<=*pattern*)	Positive lookbehind assertion: ensures that the preceding characters match pattern, but doesn't include those characters in the matched text
(?<!*pattern*)	Negative lookbehind assertion: ensures that the preceding characters do not match pattern, but doesn't include those characters in the matched text
(?>*subexp*	Atomic group (don't backtrack in subexp)
(?<name>*subexp*) [or] (?'name'*sub exp*)	Named group

Back references. Table 33 shows back referencing options.

Table 33. Back references in Ruby regular expressions

Reference	Description
n	Back reference by group number (*n* >= 1)
\\k*n*	Back reference by group number (*n* >= 1)
\\k'*n*'	Back reference by group number (*n* >= 1)
\\k*n*	Back reference by relative group number (*n* >= 1)
\\k'-*n*'	Back reference by relative group number (*n* >= 1)

Reference	Description
\k<*name*>	Back reference by group name
\k'*name*'	Back reference by group name

Subexpression calls. Table 34 lists options for calling subexpressions.

Table 34. Subexpression calls in Ruby regular expressions

Call	Description
\g<*name*>	Call by group name
\g'*name*'	Call by group name
\g*n*	Call by group number (*n* >= 1)
\g'*n*'	Call by group number (*n* >= 1)
\g-*n*	Call by relative group number (*n* >= 1)
\g'-*n*'	Call by relative group number (*n* >= 1)

String Methods

Following are the public String methods, adapted and abbreviated from *http://www.ruby-doc.org/core-2.2.2/String.html*, and formatted and printed here for your convenience.

Public class methods

```
String.new(string = "")
```
Returns new string containing copy of string.

```
String.try_convert(object)
```
Tries to convert object into string using String#to_str. Returns converted string or nil if object cannot be converted for any reason.

Public instance methods

string % argument

Uses `string` as format specification, returns `string` result of applying `argument`. If format specification contains more than one substitution, `argument` must be Array or Hash containing values to be substituted. See `Kernel#sprintf` for details.

*string * integer*

Returns new string containing integer number of copies of `string`. `integer` must be greater than or equal to 0.

string + other_string

Returns new string containing `other_string` concatenated to `string`.

string << integer

Concatenates (appends) given object to `string`. If object is `integer`, considered codepoint and is converted to character before concatenation.

string <=> other_string

Returns `-1`, `0`, `+1`, or `nil`, depending on whether `string` is less than, equal to, or greater than `other_string`, `nil` if values are incomparable.

string == object

Returns `true` if string == object, otherwise `false`. If object is not instance of `String` but responds to `to_str`, then strings are compared using case equality—that is, `Object#===`; otherwise, returns similarly to `#eql?`, comparing length and content. Compare `String#===` and `Object#===`.

string === object

Returns `true` if string == object; otherwise, `false`. Typically overridden by descendants to provide meaningful semantics in case statements. Compare `String#==` and `Object#==`.

string =~ object

> If object is regular expression, use as pattern to match against string, returning position where match starts, nil if no match. Otherwise, invokes object.=~, passing string as argument. Default =~ in Object returns nil.

string[index] **[or]** *string[start, length]* **[or]**
string[range] **[or]** *string[regexp]* **[or]**
string[regexp, capture] **[or]** *string[match_string]*

> If passed single index, returns substring of one character at that index. If passed start index and length, returns substring containing length characters, starting at index. If passed range, its beginning and end are interpreted as offsets delimiting substring to be returned. If index negative, counted from end of string. For start and range cases, start is just before character and index matching string's size. Empty string returned when start for character range is at end of string. Returns nil if initial index falls outside string or length negative.

> If regular expression supplied, matching portion of string returned. If capture follows regular expression, which may be capture group index or name, that component of MatchData is returned instead. If match_string given, that string is returned if it occurs in string. Returns nil if regular expression does not match or match string not found.

string[*fixnum*]= *new_string* **[or]** *string*[*fixnum*, *fixnum*]= *new_string* **[or]** *string*[*range*]= *aString* **[or]** *string*[*regexp*]= *new_string* **[or]** *string*[*regexp*, *fixnum*]= *new_string* **[or]** *string*[*regexp*, *name*]= *new_string* **[or]** *string*[*other_str*]= *new_string*

Replaces (assigns) some or all of content of string. Portion of string affected is determined using same criteria as String#[]. If replacement string is not same length as text it is replacing, string adjusted accordingly. If regular expression or string is used as index and it doesn't match position in string, IndexError is raised. If regular expression form is used, optional second fixnum allows you to specify which portion of match to replace. Forms that take fixnum will raise IndexError if value is out of range; range form will raise RangeError, and Regexp and String forms raise IndexError on negative match.

string.ascii_only?

Returns true for string that has only ASCII characters, false otherwise.

string.b

Returns copied string with ASCII-8BIT encoding.

string.block_scanf

Scans current string until match is exhausted, yielding each match as encountered in string. Block not necessary as results will simply be aggregated into array. (Must require scanf library with Kernel#require.)

string.bytes

Returns array of bytes in string (shorthand for *string*.each_byte.to_a). If block given, which is deprecated form, works same as String#each_byte.

string.bytesize

Returns length of string in bytes. Compare String#length and String#size.

string.byteslice(*fixnum*) **[or]** *string*.byteslice(*fixnum*, *fixnum*) **[or]** *string*.byteslice(*range*)

> If passed single fixnum, returns substring of one byte at that position; if passed two fixnums, returns substring starting at offset given by first, length given by second; if given range, returns substring containing bytes at offsets given by range. If offset is negative, counted from end of string. Returns nil if initial offset falls outside string, length is negative, or beginning of range is greater than end. Encoding remains original.

string.capitalize

> Returns copy of string with first character converted to uppercase, and remainder lowercase. Case conversion effective only in ASCII region. Compare String#capitalize!.

string.capitalize!

> Modifies string in place by converting first character to uppercase; remainder, lowercase; nil if no changes made. Case conversion effective only in ASCII region. Compare String#capitalize.

string.casecmp(*other_string*)

> Case-insensitive version of String#<=>. Compare String#<=>.

string.center(*width, padstring*=' ')

> Centers string in width. If width greater than length of string, returns new string of length width with string centered and padded with padstring; otherwise, returns string.

string.chars

> Returns array of characters from string (shorthand for string.each_char.to_a). If block is given, which is deprecated form, works same as String#each_char.

string.chomp(*separator* = $/)

> Returns new string with given record separator removed from end of string (if present). If $/ has not been changed from default Ruby record separator, chomp also removes carriage return characters (\n, \r, and \r\n). If $/ is empty string, removes all trailing newlines from string. Compare String#chop and String#chomp!.

string.chomp!(*separator* = $/)

> Modifies string in place as described in String#chomp, returning string, or nil if no modifications made. Compare with String#chomp and String#chop.

string.chop

> Returns new string with last character removed. If string ends with \r\n, both characters removed. Applying chop to empty string returns an empty string. String#chomp is often safer alternative, as it leaves string unchanged if it doesn't end in record separator. Compare with String#chomp and String#chop!.

string.chop!

> Processes string as for String#chop, returning string or nil if string empty. Compare with String#chop and String#chomp!.

string.chr

> Returns one-character string at beginning of string.

string.clear

> Makes string empty.

string.codepoints

> Returns array of integer ordinals of characters in string. Shorthand for string.each_codepoint.to_a. If block given, which is deprecated form, works same as String#each_codepoint.

string.concat(*integer*) **[or]** *string*.concat(*object*)

Concatenates (appends) given object to string. If object is integer, it is considered as codepoint and converted to character before concatenation.

string.count(*other_string*, . . .)

Each other_string, one or more, defines set of characters to count. Intersection of these sets defines characters to count in string. Any other_string that starts with caret (^) is negated. Sequence c1-c2 means all characters between c1 and c2. Backslash character (\) can be used to escape caret (^) or dash (-) and is otherwise ignored unless it appears at end of sequence or end of other_string.

string.crypt(*salt_string*)

Applies one-way cryptographic hash to string by invoking standard library function crypt(3) with given salt_string. While format and result are system and implementation dependent, using salt that matches regular expression \A[a-zA-Z0-9./]{2} should be valid and safe on any platform in which only first two characters are significant.

string.delete(*other_string*, . . .)

Returns copy of string with all characters in intersection of other_string (one or more) deleted. Uses same rules for building set of characters as String#count. Compare with String#delete!.

string.delete!(*other_string*, . . .)

Performs delete operation in place, returning string, or nil if string was not modified. Compare with String#delete.

string.downcase

Returns copy of string with all uppercase letters replaced with their lowercase counterparts. Operation is locale-insensitive—only characters *A* to *Z* affected. Case replace-

ment is effective only in ASCII region. Compare with
String#downcase!.

string.downcase!

Downcases contents of string, returning nil if no changes
were made. Note that case replacement is effective only in
ASCII region. Compare with String#downcase.

string.dump

Produces version of string with all non-printing characters replaced by \nnn notation and all special characters
escaped.

string.each_byte **[or]** *string*.each_byte { |fixnum| block }

Passes each byte in string to given block, or returns enumerator if no block given.

string.each_char **[or]** *string*.each_char { |cstr| block }

Passes each character in string to given block, or returns
enumerator if no block given.

string.each_codepoint **[or]**

string.each_codepoint { |integer| block }

Passes integer ordinal of each character in string, also
known as codepoint when applied to Unicode strings, to
given block. If no block given, enumerator returned
instead.

string.each_line(*separator* = $/) **[or]**

string.each_line(*separator* = $/) { |*substr*| *block* }

Splits string using supplied parameter as record separator
($/ by default), passing each substring in turn to supplied
block. If zero-length record separator supplied, string is
split into paragraphs delimited by multiple successive
newlines. If no block, returns enumerator.

string.empty?

Returns true if string has length of zero.

string.encode([*options*]) **[or]** *string*.encode(*encoding* [,
options]) **[or]** *string*.encode(*dst_encoding*, *src_encoding*
[, *options*])

First form returns copy of `string` transcoded to `Encod
ing#default_internal`, depending on `options`. Next form
returns copy of `string`, transcoded to `encoding`. Last form
returns copy of `string`, transcoded from `src_encoding` to
`dst_encoding`. Options are as follows:

:invalid

> If value is :replace, encode replaces invalid byte
> sequences in string with replacement character.
> Default is to raise `Encoding.InvalidByteSequenceEr
> ror` exception.

:undef

> If value is :replace, encode replaces characters
> that are undsefined in destination encoding with
> replacement character. Default is to raise
> `Encoding.UndefinedConversionError`.

:replace

> Sets replacement `string` to given value. Default
> replacement string is uFFFD for Unicode encoding
> forms; ? otherwise.

:fallback

> Sets replacement `string` by given object for unde-
> fined character. Object should be hash, proc, method,
> or an object that has [] method. Its key is undefined
> character encoded in source encoding of current
> transcoder. Its value can be any encoding until it can
> be converted into destination encoding of transcoder.

:xml

> Value must be :text or :attr. If value is :text,
> encode replaces undefined characters with their
> (uppercase hexadecimal) numeric character refer-
> ences. The &, <, and > characters are converted to
> &, <, and >, respectively. If value is :attr,

encode also quotes replacement result (using "), and replaces " with ".

:cr_newline
Replaces LF (n) with CR (r) if value is true.

:crlf_newline
Replaces LF (n) with CRLF (rn) if value is true.

:universal_newline
Replaces CRLF (rn) and CR (r) with LF (n) if value is true.

string.encode!(*encoding, options*) **[or]** *string*.encode!
(*dst_encoding, src_encoding, options*)

First form transcodes contents of string from string.encoding to encoding; second form transcodes contents of string from src_encoding to dst_encoding; options gives details for conversion. See String#encode for details. Returns string even if no changes made.

string.encoding

Returns encoding object that represents encoding of string.

string.end_with?(*suffix, . . .*)

Returns true if string ends with one or more suffixes given.

string.eql?(*other_string*)

Two strings are equal if they have same length and content.

string.ext(*new_extension*)

Replace file extension with new_extension. If there is no extension on string, append new_extension to end. If new_extension not given or empty, remove existing extension. (String#ext is user-added method for String class from Rake.)

string.force_encoding(*encoding*)

Changes encoding to encoding, returns string.

string.getbyte(*index*)

Returns indexth byte as integer, in range 0 through 255.

string.gsub(*pattern*) **[or]** *string*.gsub(*pattern*, *replacement*) **[or]** *string*.gsub(*pattern*, *hash*) **[or]** *string*.gsub(*pattern*) { |*match*| *block* }

Returns copy of string with all occurrences of pattern substituted for second argument. Pattern is typically a regular expression (Regexp); if given as string, any regular expression metacharacters it contains are interpreted literally; for example, \d will match backlash followed by d instead of digit.

If replacement is string, it will be substituted for matched text. May contain back-references to pattern's capture groups of form \d, where d is group number; or \k*n*, where n is group name. If it is double-quoted string, both back-references must be preceded by an additional backslash. However, within replacement, special match variables, such as $&, will not refer to current match. If second argument is hash and matched text is one of its keys, corresponding value is replacement string.

In block form, current match string is passed in as parameter, and variables such as $1, $2, $`, $&, and $' will be set appropriately. Value returned by block will be substituted for match on each call. Result inherits any tainting in original string or any supplied replacement string. When neither block nor second argument are supplied, returns enumerator. Compare String#gsub!.

string.gsub!(*pattern*) **[or]** *string*.gsub!(*pattern*, *replacement*) **[or]** *string*.gsub!(*pattern*) { |*match*| *block* }

Performs substitutions of String#gsub in place, returning string, or nil if no substitutions were performed. If no block or replacement given, returns enumerator. Compare with `String#gsub`.

string.hash

Return hashcode based on `string`'s length, content, and encoding. Compare with `Object#hash`.

string.hex

Treats leading characters from `string` as string of hexadecimal digits (with optional sign and optional `0x`) and returns corresponding number. Zero returned on error.

string.include?(*other_string*)

Returns `true` if `string` contains given string or character, `false` otherwise.

string.index(*substring, offset*) **[or]** *string*.index(*regexp, offset*)

Returns index of first occurrence of given substring or regular expression pattern (`Regexp`) in `string`. Returns `nil` if not found. If second parameter present, specifies position in string to begin search.

string.insert(*index, other_string*)

Inserts `other_string` before character at given index, modifying `string`. Negative indices count from end of string, and insert after given character. Intent is insert string so that it starts at given index.

string.inspect

Returns printable version of `string`, surrounded by quote marks, with special characters escaped. Compare with `String#to_str`.

string.intern

Returns symbol corresponding to `string`, creating symbol if it did not previously exist. This can also be used to create symbols that cannot be represented using `:sym` notation. Compare with `Symbol#id2name` and `String#to_sym`.

string.iseuc

> Returns true if string's encoding is EUC-JP, false otherwise. Compare with String#issjis and String#isutf8.

string.issjis

> Returns true if string's encoding is ISO-2022-JP, false otherwise. Compare with String#iseuc and String#isutf8.

string.isutf8

> Returns true if string's encoding is UTF-8, false otherwise. Compare with String#iseuc and String#issjis.

string.kconv(*to_enc, from_enc*)

> Converts string to to_enc. to_enc and from_enc are given as constants of Kconv or Encoding objects.

string.length

> Returns number of characters in string. Compare with String#bytesize and alias String#size.

string.lines(*separator* = $/)

> Returns array of lines in string split using supplied record separator ($/ by default); shorthand for string.each_line(*separator*).to_a. If block given, which is deprecated form, works same as String#each_line.

string.ljust(*integer, padstr*=' ')

> If integer is greater than length of string, returns new string of length integer with string left justified and padded with padstr; otherwise, returns string.

string.lstrip

> Returns copy of string with leading whitespace removed. Compare with String#lstrip, String#rstrip, and String#strip.

string.lstrip!

> Removes leading whitespace from string in place, returning nil if no change was made. Compare with String#lstrip, String#rstrip! and String#strip!.

string.match(*pattern*) **[or]** *string*.match(*pattern,* pos)

> Converts pattern to regular expression if it isn't already one, then invokes its match method on string. If second parameter pos present, specifies position in string to begin search. If block given, invoke block with MatchData if match succeeds.

string.next

> Returns successor to string. Successor is calculated by incrementing characters starting from rightmost alphanumeric (or rightmost character if no alphanumerics) in string. Incrementing digit always results in another digit, and incrementing letter results in another letter of same case. Incrementing nonalphanumerics uses underlying character set's collating sequence. Compare with String#next!.

string.next!

> Equivalent to String#succ, but modifies string in place. Compare with String#next.

string.oct

> Treats leading characters of string as string of octal digits (with an optional sign) and returns corresponding number. Returns 0 if conversion fails.

string.ord

> Returns integer ordinal of one-character string.

string.partition(*sep*) **[or]** *string*.partition(*regexp*)

> Searches sep or pattern (regexp) in string and returns part before it, match, and part after it. If not found, returns two empty strings and string.

string.pathmap(*spec* = nil, block)

> Map file path according to given specification, which controls details of mapping. The special patterns listed in the following table are recognized.

Specifier	Description
%p	The complete path.
%f	The base filename of the path, with its file extension, but without any directories.
%n	The filename of the path without its file extension.
%d	The directory list of the path.
%x	The file extension of the path. An empty string if there is no extension.
%X	Everything but the file extension.
%s	The alternate file separator if defined; otherwise, use #, the standard file separator.
%%	A percent sign.

The %d specifier can have a numeric prefix (for example, %2d). If number is positive, only return (up to) n directories in path, starting from lefthand side. If n negative, return (up to) n directories from righthand side of path. Compare with String#pathmap_explode, String#pathmap_partial, and String#pathmap_replace.

string.pathmap_explode

Explode path into individual components. Used by pathmap. This extension comes from Rake. Compare with String#pathmap, String#pathmap_partial, and String#pathmap_replace.

string.pathmap_partial(*n*)

Extracts partial path from path. Include n directories from the frontend (lefthand side) if n is positive, from backend (righthand side) if n negative. This extension comes from Rake. Compare with String#pathmap, String#path map_explode, and String#pathmap_replace.

string.pathmap_replace(*patterns*, *block*)

Perform pathmap replacement operations on given path pattern. Patterns take form pat1, rep1;pat2, rep2. . . .. This extension comes from Rake. Compare with String#pathmap, String#pathmap_explode, and String#pathmap_partial.

string.prepend(*other_string*)
    Prepend other_string to string.

string.replace(*other_string*)
    Replaces contents and taintedness of string with corresponding values in other_string.

string.reverse
    Returns new string with characters from string in reverse order. Compare with String#reverse!.

string.reverse!
    Reverses string in place. Compare with String#reverse.

string.rindex(*substring, fixnum*) **[or]**
string.rindex(*regexp, fixnum*)
    Returns index of last occurrence of substring or pattern (regexp) in string. Returns nil if not found. If second parameter is present, it specifies position in string to end search—characters beyond this point not considered.

string.rjust(*integer, padstr = ' '*)
    If integer is greater than length of string, returns new string of length integer with string right justified and padded with padstr; otherwise, returns string.

string.rpartition(*sep*) **[or]** *string*.rpartition(*regexp*)
    Searches sep or pattern (regexp) in string from end of string, and returns part before it, match, and part after it. If it is not found, returns two empty strings and string.

string.rstrip
    Returns copy of string with trailing whitespace removed. Compare with String#rstrip!, String#lstrip, String#strip.

string.rstrip!

Removes trailing whitespace from `string` in place, returning `nil` if no change made. Compare with `String#rstrip`, `String#lstrip!`, and `String#strip!`.

string.scan(*pattern*) **[or]** *string*.scan(*pattern*) { | *match, ...*| *block* }

Both forms iterate through `string`, matching `pattern` (which may be a regular expression or string). For each match, result is generated and either added to result array or passed to block. If pattern contains no groups, each individual result consists of matched string (`$&`). If pattern contains groups, each individual result is itself array containing one entry per group.

string.scanf(*format_string*) { |*current_match*| *block* }

Scans current `string` for match via `format_string`. If a block given, functions exactly like `String#block_scanf`. Must require scanf to use this method. Compare with `String#block_scanf`.

string.scrub **[or]** *string*.scrub(*replace*) **[or]** *string*.scrub { |*bytes*| }

If `string` is invalid byte sequence, replace invalid bytes with given `replace` character, else returns `string`. If block given, replace invalid bytes with return values of block.

string.scrub! **[or]** *string*.scrub!(*repl*) **[or]** *string*.scrub! { |*bytes*| }

If `string` is invalid byte sequence, replaces invalid bytes with given replacement character, string returns `string`. If block given, replace invalid bytes with return values of block.

string.setbyte(*index, integer*)

Modifies `index`th byte as integer.

string.shellescape

Escapes `string` so it can be safely used in Bourne shell command line. Compare with `String#shellsplit`.

string.shellsplit

> Splits `string` into array of tokens, in same way Unix Bourne shell does. Compare with `String#shellescape`.

string.size

> Returns number of characters in `string`. Compare with `String#bytesize` and alias `String#length`.

string.slice(*index*) **[or]** *string*.slice(*start, length*) **[or]**
string.slice(*range*) **[or]** *string*.slice(regexp) **[or]**
string.slice(*regexp, capture*) **[or]**
string.slice(*match_string*)

> If passed single `index`, returns substring of one character at that index. If passed `start` index and `length`, returns substring containing `length` characters from `start`. If passed `range`, its beginning and end are interpreted as off-sets delimiting substring to be returned. If `index` is negative, it is counted from end of `string`. For `start` and `range` cases, `start` is just before character and index matching `string`'s size. Returns empty string when `start` of character range is at end of `string`. Returns `nil` if initial `index` falls outside string or `length` is negative.
>
> If regular expression supplied, matching portion of `string` is returned. If `capture` follows regular expression, which may be capture group index or name, that component of `MatchData` is returned instead. If `match_string` is given, that string is returned if it occurs in `string`. Returns `nil` if regular expression does not match or match string cannot be found. Compare with `String#slice!`.

string.slice!(*fixnum*) **[or]** *string*.slice!(*fixnum, fixnum*)
[or] *string*.slice!(*range*) **[or]** *string*.slice!(*regexp*) **[or]**
string.slice!(*other_string*)

> Deletes specified portion from `string` in place, as specified by `String#slice`, and returns portion deleted. Compare with `String#slice`.

string.split(*pattern = $;, limit*)

Divides `string` into substrings based on delimiter, returning array of substrings. If `pattern` is string, its contents are used as delimiter when splitting `string`. If `pattern` is single space, `string` is split on whitespace, with leading whitespace and runs of contiguous whitespace characters ignored.

If pattern is regular expression, `string` is divided where pattern matches. Whenever `pattern` matches zero-length string, `string` is split into individual characters. If pattern contains groups, respective matches will be returned in array as well.

string.squeeze(*other_string, . . .*)

Builds set of characters from `other_string` parameter(s) using procedure described for `String#count`. Returns new string where runs of same character that occur in this set are replaced by single character. If no arguments given, all runs of identical characters replaced by single character. Compare with `String#squeeze!`.

string.squeeze!(*other_string, . . .*)

Squeezes `string` in place, returning either `string`, or `nil` if no changes made. Compare with `String#squeeze`.

string.start_with?(*prefixes, . . .*)

Returns `true` if `string` starts with one of prefixes (one or more) given.

string.strip

Returns copy of `string` with leading and trailing whitespace removed. Compare with `String#strip!`.

string.strip!

Removes leading and trailing whitespace from `string` in place. Returns `nil` if `string` not altered. Compare with `String#strip`.

string.sub(*pattern, replacement*) **[or]** *string*.sub(*pattern, hash*) **[or]** *string*.sub(*pattern*) { |*match*| *block* }

Returns copy of string with first occurrence of pattern replaced by second argument; pattern is typically regular expression; if given as string, any regular expression meta-characters it contains will be interpreted literally; for example, \\d will match backlash followed by d, instead of digit. If replacement is string, it will be substituted for matched text. It may contain back-references to pattern's capture groups of form \d, where d is group number, or \knL, where n is group name. If it is double-quoted string, both back-references must be preceded by additional backslash. However, within replacement, special match variables, such as &$, will not refer to current match. If second argument is hash, and matched text is one of its keys, corresponding value is replacement string. In block form, current match string is passed in as parameter, and variables such as $1, $2, $`, $&, and $' will be set appropriately. Value returned by block will be substituted for match on each call. Compare with String#gsub and String#sub!.

string.sub!(*pattern, replacement*) **[or]**
string.sub!(*pattern*) { |*match*| *block* }

Performs same substitution as String#sub in place. Returns string if substitution was performed or nil if no substitution performed. Compare with String#sub and String#gsub!.

string.succ

Returns successor to string. Successor is calculated by incrementing characters starting from rightmost alphanumeric (or rightmost character if there are no alphanumerics) in string. Incrementing digit always results in another digit, and incrementing letter results in another letter of same case. Incrementing nonalphanumerics uses underlying character set's collating sequence. Compare with String#next and String#succ!.

string.succ!

> Equivalent to String#succ, but modifies string in place. Compare with String#next! and String#succ.

string.sum(*n* = 16)

> Returns basic *n*-bit checksum of characters in string, where n is optional Fixnum parameter, defaulting to 16. Result is simply sum of binary value of each byte in string *modulo $2^{**}n$ − 1*. This does not claim to be particularly good checksum.

string.swapcase

> Returns copy of string with uppercase alphabetic characters converted to lowercase and lowercase characters converted to uppercase. Case conversion is effective only in ASCII region. Compare with String#capitalize and String#swapcase!.

string.swapcase!

> Equivalent to String#swapcase, but modifies string in place, returning string, or nil if no changes made. Case conversion is effective only in ASCII region. Compare String#capitalize! and String#swapcase.

string.to_c

> Returns complex number that denotes string form. Parser ignores leading whitespaces and trailing garbage. Any digit sequences can be separated by an underscore. Returns zero for null or garbage string. Compare with Kernel#Complex.

string.to_d

> Returns string as BigDecimal. Require BigDecimal and Big Decimal/util.

string.to_f

> Returns result of interpreting leading characters in string as floating-point number. Extraneous characters past end of valid number are ignored. If there is no valid number at

start of `string`, `0.0` is returned. Method never raises an exception.

string.to_i(*base = 10*)

Returns result of interpreting leading characters in `string` as integer base `base` (between 2 and 36). Extraneous characters past end of valid number are ignored. If there is no valid number at start of string, zero (0) returned. Method never raises exception when `base` is valid.

string.to_r

Returns rational number that denotes string form. Parser ignores leading whitespace and trailing garbage. Any digit sequences can be separated by an underscore. Returns zero (0) for null or garbage string. Compare with `Kernel#Rational`.

string.to_s

Returns `string`. Compare with `String#to_str` and `String#inspect`.

string.to_str

Returns `string`. Compare with `String#to_s` and `String#inspect`.

string.to_sym

Returns symbol corresponding to `string`, creating symbol if it did not previously exist. This can also be used to create symbols that cannot be represented using `:sym` notation. Compare with `Symbol#id2name` and `String#intern`.

string.toeuc

Converts `string` to EUC-JP, returning new string.

string.tojis

Converts `string` to ISO-2022-JP, returning new string.

string.tolocale

Converts `string` to locale encoding, returning new string.

string.tosjis

    Converts `string` to SHIFT_JIS, returning new string.

string.toutf8

    Converts `string` to UTF-8, returning new string.

string.toutf16

    Converts `string` to UTF-16, returning new string.

string.toutf32

    Converts `string` to UTF-32, returning new string.

string.tr(*from_string, to_string*)

    Returns copy of `string` with characters in `from_string` replaced by corresponding characters in `to_string`. If `to_string` is shorter than `from_string`, it is padded with its last character in order to maintain correspondence. Both strings may use c1-c2 notation to denote ranges of characters, and `from_string` may start with caret (^), which denotes all characters except those listed. Backslash character \ can be used to escape ^ or - and is otherwise ignored unless it appears at end of range or end of `from_string` or `to_string`. Compare with `String#tr!`.

string.tr!(*from_string, to_string*)

    Translates `string` in place, using same rules as `String#tr`. Returns `string`, or `nil` if no changes made. Compare with `String#tr`.

string.tr_s(*from_string, to_string*)

    Processes copy of `string` as described under `String#tr`, then removes duplicate characters in regions that were affected by translation. Compare with `String#tr` and `String.tr_s!`.

string.tr_s!(*from_string, to_string*)

    Performs `String#tr_s` processing on `string` in place, returning `string`, or `nil` if no changes were made. Compare with `String#tr` and `String#tr_s`.

string.unicode_normalize(*form* = :*nfc*)

Returns normalized form of string, using Unicode normalizations NFC, NFD, NFKC, or NFKD. Normalization form used determined by form, which is any of the four values: :nfc (default), :nfd, :nfkc, or :nfkd. Compare with String#unicode_normalize! and String#unicode_normalized?.

string.unicode_normalize!

Normalizes string in place, according to String#unicode_normalize. Compare with String#unicode_normalize and String#unicode_normalized?.

string.unicode_normalized?

Checks whether string is in Unicode normalization form form, which is any of the four values representing Unicode normalizations: :nfc (default), :nfd, :nfkc, or :nfkd. Compare with String#unicode_normalize.

string.unpack(*format*)

Decodes string (which may contain binary data) according to format string, returning an array of each value extracted. Format string consists of sequence of single-character directives, summarized in table. Each directive may be followed by number, indicating number of times to repeat with this directive. An asterisk (*) will use up all remaining elements. Directives sSiIlL may each be followed by an underscore (_) or exclamation mark (!) to use underlying platform's native size for specified type; otherwise, it uses platform-independent consistent size. Spaces are ignored in format string. Compare with Array#pack.

This table summarizes various formats and Ruby classes returned by each. Compare these tables with the one for Array#pack (Table 35), which is organized alphabetically (roughly).

Integer Directives	Returns	Description
C	Integer	8-bit unsigned (unsigned char).
S	Integer	16-bit unsigned, native endian (uint16_t).
L	Integer	32-bit unsigned, native endian (uint32_t).
Q	Integer	64-bit unsigned, native endian (uint64_t).
c	Integer	8-bit signed (signed char).
s	Integer	16-bit signed, native endian (int16_t).
l	Integer	32-bit signed, native endian (int32_t).
q	Integer	64-bit signed, native endian (int64_t).
S_ , S!	Integer	Unsigned short, native endian.
I, I_, I!	Integer	Unsigned int, native endian.
L_ , L!	Integer	Unsigned long, native endian.
Q_ , Q!	Integer	Unsigned long long, native endian (ArgumentError if platform has no long long type). Q_ and Q! available since Ruby 2.1.
s_ , s!	Integer	Signed short, native endian.
i, i_, i!	Integer	Signed int, native endian.
l_ , l!	Integer	Signed long, native endian.
q_ , q!	Integer	Signed long long, native endian (ArgumentError if platform has no long long type.) q_ and q! available since Ruby 2.1.
S> L> Q>	Integer	Same as directives without > except big endian.
s> l> q>		
S!> I!>		(Available since Ruby 1.9.3)
L!> Q!>		S> is same as n.
s!> i!>		L> is same as N.
l!> q!>		
S< L< Q<	Integer	Same as directives without < except little endian.

Integer Directives	Returns	Description
s< l< q<		
S!< I!<		(Available since Ruby 1.9.3).
L!< Q!<		S< is same as v.
s!< i!<		L< is same as V.
l!< q!<		
n	Integer	16-bit unsigned, network (big endian) byte order.
N	Integer	32-bit unsigned, network (big endian) byte order.
v	Integer	16-bit unsigned, VAX (little endian) byte order.
V	Integer	32-bit unsigned, VAX (little endian) byte order.
U	Integer	UTF-8 character.
w	Integer	BER-compressed integer (compare Array#pack).

Float Directives	Returns	Description
D, d	Float	Double-precision, native format.
F, f	Float	Single-precision, native format.
E	Float	Double-precision, little-endian byte order.
e	Float	Single-precision, little-endian byte order.
G	Float	Double-precision, network (big-endian) byte order.
g	Float	Single-precision, network (big-endian) byte order.

String Directives	Returns	Description
A	String	Arbitrary binary string (remove trailing nulls and ASCII spaces).
a	String	Arbitrary binary string.
Z	String	Null-terminated string.
B	String	Bit string (MSB first).
b	String	Bit string (LSB first).

String Directives	Returns	Description
H	String	Hex string (high nibble first).
h	String	Hex string (low nibble first).
u	String	UU-encoded string.
M	String	Quoted-printable, MIME encoding (see RFC2045).
m	String	Base64-encoded string (see RFC 2045) (default).
m		Base64-encoded string (see RFC 4648) if followed by 0.
P	String	Pointer to structure (fixed-length string).
p	String	Pointer to null-terminated string.

Miscellaneous Directives	Returns	Description
@	None	Skip to offset given by length argument.
X	None	Skip backward one byte.
x	None	Skip forward one byte.

string.upcase

Returns copy of string with all lowercase letters replaced with uppercase counterparts. Operation is locale-insensitive—only characters *a* to *z* are affected. Case replacement effective only in ASCII region.

string.upcase!

Upcases contents of string in place, returning nil if no changes made. Case replacement is effective only in ASCII region.

string.upto(*other_string*, *exclusive* = *false*) **[or]**
string.upto(*other_string*, *exclusive* = *false*) { |*s*| *block* }

Iterates through successive values, starting at string and ending at other_string inclusive, passing each value in turn to block. String#succ method is used to generate each value. If optional second argument `exclusive` omitted or `false`, last value included; otherwise, will be excluded. If no block, returns enumerator. If `string` and `other_string` contain only ASCII numeric characters, both are recognized as decimal numbers. In addition, width of `string` (with, for example, leading zeros) handled appropriately.

string.`valid_encoding?`

Returns `true` for string that is encoded correctly.

Array Class

The `Array` class is one of Ruby's built-in collection classes. Arrays are compact, ordered collections of objects. Ruby arrays can hold objects such as `String`, `Integer`, `Fixnum`, `Hash`, `Symbol`, even other `Array` objects. Any object that Ruby can create, it can hold in an array. Each element in an array is associated with and referred to by an *index*, sometimes known as a *subscript* in other languages. Array elements are automatically indexed (numbered) with an integer (`Fixnum`), starting with `0`, then numbered consecutively, adding `1` for each additional element. In certain instances, you can refer to the last element of an array with `-1`, the second to last with `-2`, and so forth. Ruby arrays are not as rigid as arrays in other languages. With static, compiled programming languages, you have to guess the ultimate size of the array at the time it is created. Not so with Ruby —arrays grow automatically.

Creating Arrays

There are many ways to create or initialize an array. One way is with the `new` class method:

```
months = Array.new
```

You can set the size of an array (the number of elements in an array) with an argument:

```
months = Array.new(12) [or] months = Array.new 12
```

The array months now has a size (length) of 12 elements. You can return the size of an array with either the size or length methods:

```
months.size # => 12 [or] months.length # => 12
```

Another form of new lets you assign an object such as a string to each element in the array:

```
month = Array.new(12, "month")
```

You can also use a block with new, populating each element with what the block evaluates to:

```
num = Array.new(10) { |e| e = e * 2 }
```

This yields an array of even numbers:

```
[0, 2, 4, 6, 8, 10, 12, 14, 16, 18]
```

Another Array class method, [], initializes an array like this:

```
month_abbrv = Array.[]( "jan", "feb", "mar", "apr", "may",
    "jun", "jul", "aug", "sep", "oct", "nov", "dec" )
```

Or by dropping the period or "dot" (.) and parentheses (( )), which is possible because of Ruby's flexible method syntax:

```
month_abbrv = Array[ "jan", "feb", "mar", "apr", "may",
    "jun", "jul", "aug", "sep", "oct", "nov", "dec" ]
```

An even simpler method for creating an array is by using only the square brackets (notice nil is not quoted):

```
months = [ nil, "January", "February", "March", "April",
    "May", "June", "July", "August", "September", "October",
    "November", "December" ]
```

The Kernel module, included in Object, has an Array method that only accepts a single argument. Here the method takes a range as an argument to create an array of digits:

```
digits = Array(0..9) # => [1, 2, 3, 4, 5, 6, 7, 8, 9]
```

With the %w notation, you can define an array of strings. It assumes that all elements are strings—even nil—while saving keystrokes (no quotes or commas):

```
months = %w[ nil January February March April May June
   July August September October November December ]
```

To fill an array with numbers as strings using %w, follow this syntax:

```
year = %w[ 2010 2011 2012 2013 2014 2015 2016 2017
   2018 2019 ]
```

As numbers (not strings), use this:

```
year = [2010, 2011, 2012, 2013, 2014, 2015, 2016, 2017,
   2018, 2019]
```

You can even have an array that contains objects from different classes, not all just one type. For example, here's an array that contains four elements, each a different kind of object:

```
hodge_podge = ["January", 1, :year, [2025,01,01]]
```

Following are the public class and instance methods of the Array class, adapted and abbreviated from *http://www.ruby-doc.org/core-2.2.2/Array.html*, where you will find examples and more detailed explanations of these methods.

Array Class Methods

Array.[](. . .) **[or]** Array[. . .] **[or]** [...]
   Returns a new array populated with given objects.

Array.new(*size* = 0, *object* = nil) **[or]** Array.new(*array*)
[or] Array.new(*size*) { |*index*| *block* }
   Returns new array. In first form, new array is empty. In the second, it is created with *size* copies of *object* (that is, *size* references to the same *object*). Third form creates copy of array passed as parameter. In last form, array of given *size* is created. Each element in this array is calculated by passing element's index to given block and storing return value.

```
Array.try_convert(object)
```
Tries to convert object into array, using to_ary instance method. Returns converted array or nil if object cannot be converted for any reason.

Array Instance Methods

array & *other_array*

Returns new array with elements common to both but no duplicates.

array * *integer* **[or]** *array* * *string*

Returns new array by concatenating *integer* copies of self, or with *string* argument, equivalent to self.join(string).

array + *other_array*

Returns new array by concatenation of arrays.

array - *other_array*

Returns new copy of array, removing any items that also appear in other_array. Order of array preserved.

array | *other_array*

Set union. Returns new array by joining array with other_array, excluding duplicates and preserving order. Compare with Array#uniq.

array << *object*

Pushes object onto end of array. Returns array itself. Several appends may be chained together.

array <=> *other_array*

Returns integer if array is less than (-1), equal to (0), or greater than (+1) other_array.

array == *other_array*

Arrays are equal if they contain same number of elements and each element is equal to its corresponding element.

array[*index*] **[or]** *array*[*start, length*] **[or]** *array*[*range*]
[or] *array*.slice(*index*) **[or]** *array*.slice(*start, length*)
[or] *array*.slice(*range*)

Returns element at `index`, or returns subarray starting at the `start` index and continuing for `length` elements, or returns subarray specified by `range` of indices. Negative indices count backward from end of array (`-1` is the last element). For `start` and `range` cases, starting `index` is just before element. Additionally, empty array is returned when starting `index` for element range is at end of array. Returns `nil` if `index` (or `start`) are out of range.

array[*index*]= *object* **[or]** *array*[*start, length*]= *object*|
an_array|*nil* **[or]** *array*[*range*]= *object*|*an_array*|*nil*

Sets element at `index`, or replaces subarray from `start` index for `length` elements, or replaces subarray specified by `range` of indices. If indices are greater than current capacity of array, array grows automatically. Elements are inserted into array at `start` if `length` is zero. Negative indices count backward from end of array. For `start` and `range` cases, `start` index is just before element. Compare with `Array#push` and `Array#unshift`.

array.abbrev(*pattern = nil*)

Calculates set of unambiguous abbreviations for strings in `array`. Optional `pattern` parameter is pattern or string. Only input strings that match `pattern` or start with string are included in output (hash). Must require abbrev.

array.any? { |*object*| *block* }

Passes each element of `array` to block. Returns `true` if block ever returns a value other than `false` or `nil`. If block not given, Ruby adds implicit block of { |*object*| *object* } that causes method to return `true` if at least one collection member is not `false` or `nil`.

array.assoc(*object*)

Searches through `array` whose elements are also arrays, comparing `object` with first element of each contained array using `object.==`. Returns first contained array that matches (that is, the first associated array), or `nil` if no match found. Compare with `Array#rassoc`.

array.at(*index*)
> Returns element at `index`, `nil` if out of range. Negative index counts from end of `array`. Compare with `Array#[]`.

array.bsearch { |x| *block* }
> Binary search. Finds value from `array` that meets given condition in O(`log n`) where `n` is the size of `array`.

array.clear
> Deletes all elements from `array`.

array.collect **[or]** *array*.collect { |*item*| *block* }
> Invokes block once for each element in `array`, creating new array containing values returned by block. If no block given, enumerator returned. Compare with `Array#map`.

array.collect! **[or]** *array*.collect! { |*item*| *block* }
> Invokes block once for each element in `array`, replacing element with value returned by block. If no block given, returns enumerator. Compare with `Array#map!`.

array.combination(n) **[or]**
array.combination(n) { |c| *block* }
> When invoked with block, yields all combinations of length n of elements from `array` and returns `array` itself. If no block given, enumerator returned.

array.compact
> Returns copy of self with all `nil` elements removed.

array.compact!
> Removes `nil` elements from `array`. Returns `nil` if no changes made; otherwise, returns `array`.

array.concat *other_array*
> Appends elements of `other_array` to `array`.

array.count **[or]** *array*.count(*object*) *array*.count { |
item| *block* }

> Returns number of elements as integer. If argument given,
> counts number of elements that equal object using ==; if
> block, counts number of elements for which block returns
> true.

array.cycle(*n* = *nil*) **[or]** cycle(*n* = *nil*) { |*object*|
block }

> Calls block for each element n times or forever if nil
> given. Does nothing if non-positive number given or
> array is empty. Returns nil if loop has finished without
> getting interrupted. If no block given, enumerator
> returned.

array.dclone

> Provides unified clone operation for REXML.XPathParser to
> use across multiple object types.

array.delete(*object*) **[or]** *array*.delete(*object*) { *block* }

> Deletes items from array equal to object, nil if not found;
> if block given, returns results of block if not found.

array.delete_at(*index*)

> Deletes element at index, returning that element or nil if
> index out of range. Compare with Array#slice!.

array.delete_if { |*item*| *block* }

> Deletes every element of array for which block evaluates
> true.

array.drop(*n*)

> Drops first n elements from array and returns rest of ele-
> ments in new array. Compare with Array#take.

array.drop_while **[or]** *array*.drop_while { |*arr*| *block* }

> Drops elements up to but not including the first element
> for which block returns nil or false and returns array
> containing remaining elements. If no block given, enu-
> merator returned. Compare with Array#take_while.

array.each { |*item*| *block* }

> Calls block once for each element in array, passing element as parameter. Compare with Array#each_index.

array.each_index { |*index*| *block* }

> Calls block once for each index, passing it as parameter. Compare with Array#each.

array.empty?

> Returns true if array has no elements.

array.eql?(*other_array*)

> Returns true if array and other_array are same object or if both have same content.

array.fetch(*index*) **[or]** *array*.fetch(*index*, *default*) **[or]**
array.fetch(index) { |index| block }

> Returns element at index, but throws IndexError if out of range. Prevent this by supplying default. Alternatively, if block given, will only be executed when out-of-range index referenced. Negative index values count from the end of array.

array.fill(*object*) **[or]** *array*.fill(*object*, *range*) **[or]**
array.fill(*object*, *start* [, *length*]) **[or]** *array*.fill { |
index| *block* } **[or]** *array*.fill(*range*) { |*index*| *block* }
[or] *array*.fill(*start* [, *length*]) { |*index*| *block* }

> First three forms set selected elements of array (which may be entire array) to object; start as nil equivalent to zero; length of nil equivalent to length of array. Last three forms fill array with value of given block, which is passed absolute index of each element to be filled. Negative values of start count from the end of array, where -1 is index of last element.

array.find_index **[or]** *array*.find_index(*object*) **[or]**
array.find_index { |*item*| *block* }

> Returns index of first object in array where object is == to object. If block given, returns index of first object for

which block returns `true`. Returns `nil` if no match found. An enumerator is returned if neither block nor argument given. Compare with `Array#rindex`.

array.first **[or]** *array*.first(*n*)

Returns first element or first n elements of array. If `array` empty, first form returns `nil`, second form returns empty array. Compare with `Array#last`.

array.flatten

Returns new array as one-dimensional flattening of `array`, extracting every element of `array` into new array. Compare with `Array#flatten!`.

array.flatten!

Flattens `array` in place (no subarrays), returning `nil` if no modifcations made. Compare with `Array#flatten`.

array.frozen?

Returns `true` if `array` is frozen, even temporarily.

array.hash

Computes a hashcode for `array`. Equal arrays (as per eql?) have same hashcode.

array.include?(*object*)

Returns `true` if `object` present in `array`, otherwise `false`.

array.index(object)

Returns index of first object in `array` == to object, `nil` if no match.

array.initialize_copy(other_array)

Replaces contents of `array` with contents of other_array, truncating or expanding `array` as needed. Compare with `Array#replace`.

array.indexes

Removed. Compare with `Array#values_at`.

array.indices

Removed. Compare with `Array#values_at`.

array.insert(*index, object . . .*)

> Inserts object (or objects) at index. Negative indices count back from end of array.

array.inspect

> Returns string representation of array. Compare with Array#to_s.

array.join(*separator = $,*)

> Returns string created by converting array to string, with each element separated by separator. If separator is nil, uses current $,, default output separator; if both separator and $, are nil, uses empty string.

array.keep_if **[or]** *array*.keep_if { |*item*| *block* }

> Deletes every element in array for which block evaluates false. If no block, returns enumerator. Compare with Array#select.

array.last **[or]** *array*.last(*n*)

> Returns last element or last n elements of array. If array empty, first form returns nil, second, [ ]

array.length

> Returns number of elements in array, zero if array empty. Compare with size and Array#size.

array.map { |*item*| *block* }

> Invokes block once for each element in array, creating new array containing values returned by block. If no block given, enumerator returned. Compare with Array#collect.

array.map!

> Invokes block once for each element in array, replacing element with value returned by block. If no block given, returns enumerator. Compare with Array#collect!.

array.nitems

> Removed.

`array.pack(aTemplateString)`

Packs contents of `array` into a binary sequence according to directives in `aTemplateString` (see the following table). Directives `A`, `a`, and `Z` may be followed by a count, which gives width of resulting field. Remaining directives also may take a count, indicating number of array elements to convert. If count is asterisk (`*`), all remaining `array` elements will be converted. Any of the directives `sSiIlL` may be followed by an underscore (`_`) or exclamation mark (`!`) to use the underlying platform's native size for specified type; otherwise, they use a platform-independent size. Spaces are ignored in the template string. Compare with `String#unpack`.

Table 35 summarizes various formats and Ruby classes returned by each. Compare Table 35 with the one for `String#unpack`, which is organized by Ruby class.

Table 35. Array pack directives

Directive	Array Element	Description
@		Moves to absolute position.
A	String	Arbitrary binary string (space padded, count is width).
a	String	Arbitrary binary string (null padded, count is width).
B	String	Bit string (MSB first).
b	String	Bit string (LSB first).
C	Integer	8-bit unsigned (unsigned char).
c	Integer	8-bit signed (signed char)
D, d	Float	Double-precision, native format.
E	Float	Double-precision, little-endian byte order.
e	Float	Single-precision, little-endian byte order.

Directive	Array Element	Description
F, f	Float	Single-precision, native format.
G	Float	Double-precision, network (big-endian) byte order.
g	Float	Single-precision, network (big-endian) byte order.
H	String	Hex string (high nibble first).
h	String	Hex string (low nibble first).
I, I_, I!	Integer	Unsigned int, native endian.
i, i_, i!	Integer	Signed int, native endian.
L	Integer	32-bit unsigned, native endian (uint32_t).
L_, L!	Integer	Unsigned long, native endian.
l	Integer	32-bit signed, native endian (int32_t).
l_, l!	Integer	Signed long, native endian.
M	String	Quoted printable, MIME encoding (see RFC2045).
m	String	Base64-encoded string (see RFC 2045, count is width). If count is 0, no linefeeds are added; see RFC 4648.
N	Integer	32-bit unsigned, network (big-endian) byte order.
n	Integer	16-bit unsigned, network (big-endian) byte order.
P	String	Pointer to a structure (fixed-length string).
p	String	Pointer to a null-terminated string.
Q	Integer	64-bit unsigned, native endian (uint64_t).
Q_, Q!	Integer	Unsigned long long, native endian (ArgumentError if platform has no long long type.) Q_ and Q! have been available since Ruby 2.1.
q	Integer	64-bit signed, native endian (int64_t).
q_, q!	Integer	Signed long long, native endian (ArgumentError if platform has no long long type.) q_ and q! have been available since Ruby 2.1.

Directive	Array Element	Description
S	Integer	16-bit unsigned, native endian (uint16_t).
S< L< Q<	Integer	Same as the directives without < except little endian.
s< l< q<		
S!< I<		(Available since Ruby 1.9.3).
L!< Q!<		S< same as v.
s!< i!<		L< is same as V.
l!< q!<		
S> L> Q>	Integer	Same as the directives without > except big endian.
s> I> q>		
S!> I>		(Available since Ruby 1.9.3).
L!> Q!>		S> same as n.
s!> i!>		L> is same as N.
l!> q!>		
S_, S!	Integer	Unsigned short, native endian.
s	Integer	16-bit signed, native endian (int16_t).
s_, s!	Integer	Signed short, native endian.
U	Integer	UTF-8 character.
u	String	UU-encoded string.
V	Integer	32-bit unsigned, VAX (little-endian) byte order.
v	Integer	16-bit unsigned, VAX (little-endian) byte order.
w	Integer	BER-compressed integer.
X		Back up a byte.
x		Null byte.
Z	String	Same as a, except that null is added with *.

array.permutation **[or]** *array*.permutation { |*p*| *block* }
[or] *array*.permutation(*n*) **[or]** *array*permutation(*n*) { |*p*|
block }

> Yields all permutations of all elements in `array` when invoked with block. If n specified, yields all permutations of length n, returns self. If no block, returns enumerator.

array.pop **[or]** *array*.pop(*n*)

> Removes last element from `array` and returns it; `nil` if array empty. If n, returns array of last n elements. Compare with `Array#slice!` and `Array#push`.

array.product(*other_array*, . . .) **[or]**
array.product(*other_array*, . . .) { |*p*| *block* }

> Returns array of all combinations of elements from all arrays, one or more. If block, yields all combinations, returns self.

array.push(*object*, . . .)

> Pushes or appends `object` or objects to end of array. Several appends may be chained. Compare with `Array#pop`.

array.rassoc(*key*)

> Searches `array` whose elements are also arrays, comparing `object` with second element of each contained array using `object.==`. Returns first contained array that matches `object`. Compare with `Array#assoc`.

array.reject **[or]** *array*.reject { |*item*| *block*}

> Returns new array containing items in `array` for which block not `true`; `nil` if no change. If no block, returns enumerator. Compare with `Array#delete_if`.

array.reject! **[or]** *array*.reject! { |*item*| *block*}

> Deletes elements from `array` for which block evaluates `true`, `nil` if no change. Equivalent to `Array#delete_if`. Compare with `Array#reject`.

array.repeated_combination(*n*) **[or]**

array.repeated_combination(*n*) { |*c*| *block* }

> When invoked with block, yields all repeated combinations of length n of elements from array, then returns array itself. If no block, returns enumerator. Compare with Array#repeated_permutation.

array.repeated_permutation(*n*) **[or]**

array.repeated_permutation(*n*) { |*c*| *block* }

> When invoked with block, yields all repeated permutations of length n of elements from array, then returns array itself. If no block, returns enumerator. Compare with Array#repeated_combination.

array.replace(*other_array*)

> Replaces contents of array with contents of other_array, truncating or expanding array as needed. Compare with Array#initialize_copy.

array.reverse

> Returns new array containing array's elements in reverse order. Compare with Array#reverse!.

array.reverse!

> Reverses array in place. Compare with Array#reverse.

array.reverse_each **[or]** *array*.reverse_each { |*item*| *block* }

> Same as Array#each but traverses array in reverse order.

array.rindex **[or]** *array*.rindex(*object*) **[or]** *array*.rindex { |*item*| *block* }

> Returns index of last object in *array* == to *object*. If block, returns index of first object for which block returns true, starting from last object; nil if no match. If no argument or block, returns enumerator. Compare with Array#index.

array.rotate(*count*)

> Returns new array by rotating array so that element at count is first element of new array. Compare with Array#rotate!.

array.rotate!(*count*)

> Rotates array in place so element at count comes first, then returns self. If count negative, starts from end of array (last element is -1).

array.sample **[or]** *array*.sample(*random: rng*) **[or]**

array.sample(*n*) **[or]** *array*.sample(*n, random: rng*)

> Chooses random element or random number n of elements from array. Optional rng argument used as random number generator. If empty, first form returns nil, second, empty array.

array.select **[or]** *array*.select { |*item*| *block* }

> Returns new array containing all elements of array for which block returns true. If no block, returns enumerator. Compare with Array#select!.

array.select! **[or]** *array*.select! { |*item*| *block* }

> Invokes block, passing in elements from array, deleting elements for which block returns false. If no block, returns enumerator. Compare with Array#select and Array#keep_if.

array.shelljoin

> Builds command-line string from argument list array, joining all elements escaped for the Bourne shell and separated by space.

array.shift **[or]** *array*.shift(*n*)

> Removes first element of array, or first n number of elements, and returns them, shifting all other elements down by one, nil if array empty.

array.shuffle **[or]** *array*.shuffle(*random: rng*)

> Returns new array with elements of array shuffled. Optional rng argument used as random number generator.

array.shuffle! **[or]** *array*.shuffle!(*random: rng*)

> Shuffles elements of array in place. Optional rng argument used as random number generator.

array.size

> Returns number of elements in array, zero if array empty. Compare with Array#length.

array.slice(*index*) **[or]** *array*.slice(*start, length*) **[or]**
array.slice(*range*)

> Returns element at index, or subarray at start and continuing for length, or returns subarray specified by range of indices. Returns nil if index or start out of range. Negative indices count backward from end of array (-1 is last element). For start and range, start is just before element. Returns empty array when start for element range at end of array. Compare with Array#[] and Array#slice!.

array.slice!(*index*) **[or]** *array*.slice!(*start, length*)
[or] *array*.slice!(*range*)

> Deletes element or elements specified by index, start and length, or range. Compare with Array#slice.

array.sort **[or]** *array*.sort { |*a, b*| *block* }

> Returns new array created by sorting array. Compare with Array#sort!.

array.sort! **[or]** *array*.sort! { |*a, b*| *block* }

> Sorts array in place. Compare with Array#sort.

array.sort_by! **[or]** *array*.sort_by! { |*object*| *block* }

> Sorts array in place using set of keys generated by mapping values in array through block. If no block, returns enumerator.

array.take(n)

> Returns first n elements in array. Compare with Array#drop and Array#take_while.

array.take_while **[or]** *array*.take_while { |*array*| *block* }

> Passes elements to block until it returns nil or false, then stops and returns array of all prior elements. If no block, returns enumerator. Compare with Array#take and Array#drop_while.

array.to_a

> Returns array (self). If called on subclass of Array, converts receiver to Array object. Compare with Array#to_ary.

array.to_ary

> Returns array (self). Compare with Array#to_a.

array.to_h

> Returns hash by interpreting array containing subarrays of key-value pairs.

array.to_s

> Returns string representation of array. Compare with Array#inspect.

array.transpose

> Transposes array's rows and columns, assuming array is array of arrays.

array.uniq **[or]** *array*.uniq { |*item*| . . . }

> Returns new array without duplicate values from array. If block, uses return values of block for comparison. Compare with Array#uniq!.

array.uniq! **[or]** *array*.uniq! { |*item*| . . .}

> Removes duplicate values from array. If block given, uses return values of block for comparison. Compare with Array#uniq.

array.unshift(*object*, . . .)

> Prepends object or objects to front of array, moving other elements to higher indices. Compare with Array#shift.

array.values_at(*selector*, . . .)

> Returns new array containing elements in array corresponding to selector or selectors that are integer indices or ranges. Compare with Array#shift.

array.zip(*arg*, . . .) **[or]** *array*.zip(*arg*, . . .) { | *array*| *block* }

> Converts any arguments to array, merging elements of array with corresponding elements from each argument, one or more. If block, invoked for each output array; otherwise, returns array of arrays.

Hash Class

A hash is an unordered collection of key-value pairs that look like this: "storm" => "tornado". (Not the same as a hashcode. See Object#hash.) A hash is similar to an Array, but instead of a default integer index starting at zero, indexing is done with keys that can be made up from any Ruby object. In other words, you can use integer keys just like an Array, but you can use any Ruby object as a key, even an Array! (Hashes are actually implemented as arrays in Ruby.)

Hashes are accessed by keys or values. Keys must be unique. If you attempt to access a hash with a key that does not exist, the method will return nil unless the hash has a default value. The key-value pairs in a hash are not stored in the same order in which they are inserted (the order you placed them in the hash), so don't be surprised if the contents are not ordered.

Creating Hashes

There are a variety of ways to create hashes. You can create an empty hash with the new class method:

```
months = Hash.new
```

You can also use new to create a hash with a default value, which is otherwise just nil:

```
months = Hash.new( "month" ) [or] months = Hash.new "month"
```

When you access any key in a hash that has a default value, or if the key or value doesn't exist, accessing the hash will return the default value:

```
months[0] [or] months[72] [or] months[234] # => "month"
```

Hash also has a class method [], which is called in one of two ways—with a comma separating the pairs, like this (keys are symbols, values are strings):

```
christmas_carol = Hash[ :name, "Ebenezer Scrooge", :part
ner,
  "Jacob Marley", :employee, "Bob Cratchit", :location,
  "London", :year, 1843 ]
# => {:name=>"Ebenezer Scrooge", :employee=>"Bob Cratchit",
  :year=>1843, :partner=>"Jacob Marley", :location=>"Lon
don"}
```

Or with =>:

```
christmas_carol = Hash[ :name => "Ebenezer Scrooge",
  :partner => "Jacob Marley", :employee => "Bob Cratchit"
=>:location, "London", :year => 1843 ]
# => {:name=>"Ebenezer Scrooge", :employee=>"Bob Cratchit",
  :year=>1843, :partner=>"Jacob Marley", :location=>"Lon
don"}
```

The easiest way to create a hash is with curly braces. With Ruby 1.9 or later, you can also use this syntax (colon *after*):

```
numeros = { uno: 1, dos: 2, tres: 3 }
```

The spaces are optional. Here's another example using braces, but with keys and values separated by =>:

```
months = { 1 => "January", 2 => "February",
  3 => "March", 4 => "April", 5 => "May",
  6 => "June", 7 => "July", 8 => "August",
  9 => "September", 10 => "October",
  11 => "November", 12 => "December" }
```

You could use strings as keys in the following, but why not use symbols, which are more efficient?

```
month_list = { :jan => "January", :feb => "February",
  :mar => "March", :apr => "April", :may => "May",
  :jun => "June", :jul => "July", :aug => "August",
  :sep => "September", :oct => "October",
  :nov => "November", :dec => "December" }
```

Finally, you can use any Ruby object as a key or value, even an array, so even this will work: [1,"jan"] => "January".

Following are the public methods of the Hash class, adapted and abbreviated from *http://www.ruby-doc.org/core-2.2.2/ Hash.html*, where you will find examples and more detailed explanations of the methods.

Hash Class Methods

Hash[*[key (=>|,) value]**]

Creates a new hash with zero or more key-value pairs, separated by => or ,. Creates new hash with zero or more key-value pairs, separated by arrows (=>), commas (,), or colons (:) following keys.

Hash.new **[or]** Hash.new(*object*) **[or]** Hash.new {|*hash, key| block*}

Creates new, empty hash or one with default value. May also create hash via block.

Hash.try_convert(*object*)

Tries to convert object into hash, using to_hash instance method. Returns converted hash or nil if object cannot be converted for any reason.

Hash Instance Methods

hash == *other_hash*
> Tests whether two hashes are equal, based on whether they have same number of key-value pairs, and whether the key-value pairs match corresponding pair in each hash.

hash[key]
> Retrieves value associated with key. If not found, returns default value, if (see `default`, `default=`). Compare with [*key*]=.

hash[key]= value
> Assigns `value` to key in hash. Compare with `store`.

hash.any?[{|(*key,value*)| *block* }]
> Passes each element to given block. Method returns `true` if block returns value other than `false` or `nil`. If block not given, Ruby adds implicit block of { |*object*| *object* } that causes `any?` to return `true` if at least one collection member is not `false` or `nil`.

hash.assoc(object)
> Searches hash, comparing `object` with key, returning key-value pair or `nil`.

hash.clear
> Removes all key-value pairs from hash.

hash.compare_by_identity
> Compares keys in hash by identity.

hash.compare_by_identity?
> Returns `true` if hash will compare keys by identity.

hash.default(key = nil)
> Returns default value of hash.

hash.default= object
> Sets default value of hash.

hash.default_proc
> Returns block if invoked with block, otherwise nil.

hash.default_proc= *(proc_object/nil)*
> Sets default proc to execute on each failed key lookup.

hash.delete(*key*) **[or]** *hash*.delete(*key*) {| *key* | *block* }
> Deletes key-value pair, returns key; otherwise, returns default, if set.

hash.delete_if **[or]** *hash*.delete_if {| *key, value* |
block }
> Deletes every key-value pair for which block evaluates true. If no block given, returns enumerator.

hash.each **[or]** *hash*.each {| *key, value* | *block* } **[or]**
hash.each_pair **[or]** hash.each_pair {| *key, value* |
block }
> Calls block once for each key, passing key-value pair as parameters. If no block given, returns enumerator.

hash.each_key **[or]** *hash*.each_key {| *key* | *block* }
> Calls block once for each key, passing key as parameter. If no block given, returns enumerator.

hash.each_pair **[or]** *hash*.each_pair {| *key, value* |
block }
> Calls block once for each key, passing key-value pair as parameters. If no block given, returns enumerator.

hash.each_value **[or]** *hash*.each_value {| *value* | *block* }
> Calls block once for each key, passing value as parameter. If no block given, returns enumerator.

hash.empty?
> Returns true if no key-value pairs exist in hash, otherwise false.

hash.eql?(*other_hash*)
> Returns true if both hashes have same content.

hash.fetch(*key* [, *default*]) **[or]** *hash*.fetch(*key*) {| *key* | *block* }

Returns value for given key. If key not found, with no other arguments, raises KeyError exception; if default given, returns default; if block, runs and returns result.

hash.flatten **[or]** *hash*.flatten(*level*)

Returns new array—one-dimensional flattening of hash. For every key or value, extract its elements into new array. Does not flatten recursively by default; optional level argument determines level of recursion to flatten.

hash.has_key?(*key*)

Returns true if key present. Compare with include?, key?, member?.

hash.has_value?(*value*)

Returns true if value present, otherwise false. Compare with value?.

hash.hash

Computes with hashcode.

hash.include?(*key*)

Returns true if key present. Compare with has_key?, key?, and member?.

hash.indexes

Removed. Compare with select.

hash.indices

Removed. Compare with select.

hash.inspect

Returns hash as string. Compare with to_s.

hash.invert

Returns new hash, inverting keys and values.

hash.keep_if **[or]** *hash*.keep_if {|*key, value*| *block* }

Deletes every key-value pair for which block evaluates false; otherwise, returns enumerator.

hash.key(*value*)
> Returns key for value, if key present.

hash.key?(*key*)
> Returns true if key present.

hash.keys
> Returns array of keys from hash.

hash.length
> Returns number of key-value pairs. Compare with size.

hash.member?(*key*)
> Returns true if key present.

hash.merge(*other_hash*) **[or]** hash.merge(*other_hash*) {|
key,oldval,newval| *block* }
> Returns new hash with key-value pairs of both; if no block, values from duplicate keys are those of other_hash; otherwise, value of each duplicate key determined by calling block with key, value in hash and value in other_hash. Compare with update.

hash.merge!(*other_hash*) **[or]** *hash*.merge!(*other_hash*) {|
key,oldval,newval| *block* }
> Same as merge, but changes done in place.

hash.rassoc(*object*)
> Searches hash, comparing object with value using == and returning first match.

hash.rehash
> Rebuilds hash based on current hash values for each key. Recommended when you mutate a key.

hash.reject **[or]** *hash*.reject {|*key,value*| *block*}
> Returns new hash from entries for which block returns false; if no block, returns enumerator.

hash.reject! {|*key,value*| *block*}
> Same as reject, but changes made in place.

`hash.replace(other_hash)`
>   Replace contents of hash with that of `other_hash`.

hash.`select` **[or]** *hash*.`select {|`*key,value*`| block}`
>   Return new hash from entries for which block returns true; if no block, returns enumerator.

hash.`select!`
>   Same as `select`, but changes made in place.

hash.`shift`
>   Removes key-value pair and returns it as two-item array (`[ key, value ]`), or hash's default value, if empty.

hash.`size`
>   Returns number of key-value pairs. Compare with `length`.

hash.`sort` **[or]** *hash*.`sort {|`*key,value*`| block}`
>   Sorts key-value pairs in hash, returning arrays.

hash.`store(`*key, value*`)`
>   Stores, or associates, key-value pair in hash. Compare with `[]=`.

hash.`to_a`
>   Converts hash to nested array.

hash.`to_h`
>   Returns self. If called on `hash` subclass, converts receiver to hash object. Compare with `to_hash`.

hash.`to_hash`
>   Returns self. Compare with `to_h`.

hash.`to_s`
>   Returns hash as string. Compare with `inspect`.

hash.`update(`*other_hash*`)` **[or]** *hash*.`update(`*other_hash*`) {|`*key,oldval,newval*`| block}`
>   Returns new hash with key-value pairs of both; if no block, values from duplicate keys are those of `other_hash`; otherwise, value of each duplicate key determined by call-

ing block with key, value in hash and value in other_hash. Compare with `merge`, `merge!`.

hash.value?(*value*)
    Returns `true` if given value present. Compare with has_value?.

hash.values
    Returns array with values from hash.

hash.values_at(*key*[, . . .])
    Returns array containing values associated with given keys (one or more). Compare `select`, `values`.

Time Formatting Directives

The directives in Table 36 are used with the method `Time#strftime`.

Table 36. Directives for formatting time

Directive	Description
%A	Weekday name (Sunday).
%^A	Uppercased weekday name (SUNDAY).
%a	Abbreviated weekday name (Sun).
%^a	Uppercased, abbreviated weekday name (SUN).
%B	Month name (January).
%b	Abbreviated month name (Jan).
%^B	Uppercased month name (JANUARY).
%^b	Uppercased, abbreviated month name (JAN).
%C	Year / 100 (rounded down, such as 20 in 2009).
%c	Date, time (%a %b %e %T %Y).
%D	Date (%m/%d/%y).
%d	Day of month, zero-padded (01..31).
%-d	Day of month, no-padded (1..31).

Directive	Description
%e	Day of month, blank-padded (1..31).
%F	ISO 8601 date format (%Y-%m-%d).
%G	Week-based year.
%g	Last two digits of the week-based year (00..99).
%H	Hour of day, 24-hour clock, zero-padded (00..23).
%h	Equivalent to %b.
%I	Hour of the day, 12-hour clock, zero-padded (01..12).
%L	Millisecond of second (000..999). Digits under millisecond are truncated to not produce 1000.
%j	Day of year (001..366).
%k	Hour of day, 24-hour clock, blank-padded (0..23).
%l	Hour of day, 12-hour clock, blank-padded (1..12).
%M	Minute of hour (00..59).
%m	Month of year, zero-padded (01..12).
%-m	Month of year, no-padded (1..12).
%_m	Month of year, blank-padded (1..12).
%N	Fractional seconds digits, default is nine digits (nanosecond). The digits under the specified length are truncated to avoid carry up. Examples:
	• %3N millisecond (three digits)
	• %6N microsecond (six digits)
	• %9N nanosecond (nine digits)
	• %12N picosecond (12 digits)
	• %15N femtosecond (15 digits)
	• %18N attosecond (18 digits)
	• %21N zeptosecond (21 digits)
	• %24N yoctosecond (24 digits)
%n	Newline character (\n).

Directive	Description
%P	Meridian indicator, lowercase (am or pm).
%p	Meridian indicator, uppercase (AM or PM).
%R	24-hour time (%H:%M).
%r	12-hour time (%I:%M:%S %p).
%S	Second of minute (00..60).
%s	Number of seconds since 1970-01-01 00:00:00 UTC.
%T	24-hour time (%H:%M:%S).
%t	Tab character (\t).
%U	Week number of year. Week starts with Sunday (00..53).
%u	Day of week. Monday is 1 (1..7).
%V	Week number of week-based year (01..53).
%v	VMS date (%e-%^b-%4Y).
%W	Week number of year. Week starts with Monday. (00..53).
%w	Day of week. Sunday is 0 (0..6).
%X	Same as %T.
%x	Same as %D.
%Y	Year with century, if provided, will pad result at least four digits.
%y	year % 100 (00..99).
%Z	Abbreviated time zone name or similar information. (OS dependent).
%z	Time zone as hour and minute offset from UTC (e.g., +0900).
%:z	Hour, minute offset from UTC with colon (e.g., +09:00).
%::z	Hour, minute, second offset from UTC (e.g., +09:00:00).
%%	Literal % character.

Ruby Documentation

Ruby documentation refers to the documentation generated by RDoc (see *https://github.com/rdoc/rdoc* and *http://docs.seat tlerb.org/rdoc/*), a program that extracts documentation from Ruby source files, both from C and Ruby files.

The documentation is stored in comments in the source files and encoded so that RDoc can easily find it. RDoc can generate output as HTML, XML, *ri* (Ruby Interactive), or Windows help (*.chm*) files.

To see the RDoc-generated HTML documentation for Ruby on the Web, go to *http://www.ruby-doc.org/core*. If you have rdoc and Ruby documentation installed on your system, which you likely do, you can type something like the following at a shell prompt to print formatted documentation on standard output:

```
ri Kernel#print
```

You will get this output:

```
= Kernel#print

(from ruby core)
------------------------------------------------
  print(obj, ...)    -> nil
------------------------------------------------

Prints each object in turn to $stdout. If the
output field separator ($,) is not nil, its
contents will appear between each field. If the
output record separator ($\) is not nil, it will
be appended to the output. If no arguments are
given, prints $_. Objects that aren't strings will
be converted by calling their to_s method.

  print "cat", [1,2,3], 99, "\n"
  $, = ", "
  $\ = "\n"
  print "cat", [1,2,3], 99

produces:
```

```
cat12399
cat, 1, 2, 3, 99
```

The following describes the very basic RDoc version 4.2.0, and is adapted from its documentation. (See *https://github.com/rdoc/rdoc* and *http://docs.seattlerb.org/rdoc* for more information.)

Usage:

```
rdoc [options] [names, [ . . . ] ]
```

The way in which RDoc generates output depends on the output formatter being used, and on the options you give. Files are parsed and the documentation they contain collected, before any output is produced. This allows cross-references to be resolved between all files. If a name is a directory, it is traversed. If no names are specified, all Ruby files in the current directory (and subdirectories) are processed.

Options can be specified via the RDOCOPT environment variable, which functions similar to the RUBYOPT environment variable for Ruby. For example:

```
$ export RDOCOPT="--show-hash"
```

Makes RDoc show hashes in method links by default. Command-line options will always override those in RDOCOPT.

Available formatters are:

darkfish
      HTML generator, written by Michael Granger
pot
      Creates *.pot* file
ri
      Creates ri data files

RDoc understands the following file formats:

- C: \.(?:([CcHh])\1?|c([+xp])\2|y)\z
- ChangeLog: (/|\\|\A)ChangeLog[^/\\]*\z
- Markdown: \.(md|markdown)(?:\.[^.]+)?$

- RD: `\.rd(?:\.[^.]+)?$`
- Ruby: `\.rbw?$`
- Simple
- TomDoc: Only in Ruby files

The following RDoc options have been deprecated:

`--accessor`
   Support discontinued.

`--diagram`
   Support discontinued.

`--help-output`
   Support discontinued.

`--image-format`
   Was an option for `--diagram`.

`--inline-source`
   Source code is now always inlined.

`--merge`
   ri now always merges class information.

`--one-file`
   Support discontinued.

`--op-name`
   Support discontinued.

`--opname`
   Support discontinued.

`--promiscuous`
   Files always only document their content.

`--ri-system`
   Ruby installers use other techniques.

Parsing options:

-e *is preferred over* `--charset, --encoding`
> Specifies output encoding. All files read are converted to this encoding. Default is UTF-8.

`--locale=NAME`
> Specifies the output locale.

`--locale-data-dir=DIR`
> Specifies the directory where locale data live.

`-a, --all`
> Synonym for `--visibility=private`.

`-x, --exclude=PATTERN`
> Do not process files or directories matching `PATTERN`.

`-E, --extension=NEW=OLD`
> Treat files ending with *.new* as if they ended with *.old*. Using `-E cgi=rb` will cause *xxx.cgi* to be parsed as a Ruby file.

`-U, --[no-]force-update`
> Forces RDoc to scan all sources even if newer than the flag file.

`-p, --pipe`
> Convert RDoc on stdin to HTML.

`-w, --tab-width=WIDTH`
> Set the width of tab characters.

`--visibility=VISIBILITY`
> Minimum visibility to document a method. One of `public`, `protected` (the default), `private`, or `nodoc` (show everything).

`--markup=MARKUP`
> The markup format for the named files. The default is `rdoc`. Valid values are: `markdown`, `rd`, `rdoc`, `tomdoc`.

`--root=`*ROOT*

> Root of the source tree documentation will be generated for. Set this when building documentation outside the source directory. Default is the current directory.

`--page-dir=`*DIR*

> Directory in which guides, your FAQ, or other pages not associated with a class live. Set this when you don't store such files at your project root. NOTE: Do not use the same filename in the page directory and in the root of your project.

Common generator options:

`-O, --force-output`

> Forces RDoc to write the output files, even if the output directory exists and does not seem to have been created by RDoc.

`-f, --fmt, --format=`*FORMAT*

> Set the output formatter. One of: `darkfish`, `pot`, `ri`.

`-i, --include=`*DIRECTORIES*

> Set (or add to) the list of directories to be searched when satisfying `:include:` requests. Can be used more than once.

`-C[`*LEVEL*`], --[`*no-*`]coverage-report, --[`*no-*`]dcov`

> Prints a report on undocumented items. Does not generate files.

`-o, --output, --op=`*DIR*

> Set the output directory.

`-d`

> Deprecated `--diagram` option. Prevents firing debug mode with legacy invocation.

HTML generator options:

`-c, --charset=`*CHARSET*
: Specifies the output HTML character set. Use `--encoding` instead of `--charset` if available.

`-A, --hyperlink-all`
: Generate hyperlinks for all words that correspond to known methods, even if they do not start with # or :: (legacy behavior).

`-m, --main=`*NAME*
: *NAME* will be the initial page displayed.

`-N, --[`*no-*`]line-numbers`
: Include line numbers in the source code. By default, only the number of the first line is displayed, in a leading comment.

`-H, --show-hash`
: A name of the form `#name` in a comment is a possible hyperlink to an instance method name. When displayed, the # is removed unless this option is specified.

`-T, --template=`*NAME*
: Set the template used when generating output. The default depends on the formatter used.

`--template-stylesheets=`*FILES*
: Set (or add to) the list of files to include with the HTML template.

`-t, --title=`*TITLE*
: Set `TITLE` as the title for HTML output.

`--copy-files=`*PATH*
: Specify a file or directory to copy static files from. If a file is given, it will be copied into the output dir. If a directory is given, the entire directory will be copied. You can use this multiple times.

-W, --webcvs=*URL*

> Specify a URL for linking from a web frontend to CVS. If the URL contains a %s, the name of the current file will be substituted; if the URL doesn't contain a %s, the filename will be appended to it.

ri generator options:

-r, --ri

> Generate output for use by ri. The files are stored in the *.rdoc* directory under your home directory unless overridden by a subsequent --op parameter, so no special privileges are needed.

-R, --ri-site

> Generate output for use by ri. The files are stored in a site-wide directory, making them accessible to others, so special privileges are needed.

Generic options:

--write-options

> Write .rdoc_options to the current directory with the given options. Not all options will be used. See RDoc::Options for details.

--[*no*-]dry-run

> Don't write any files.

-D, --[*no*-]debug

> Displays lots of internal stuff.

--[*no*-]ignore-invalid

> Ignore invalid options and continue (default true).

-q, --quiet

> Don't show progress as we parse.

-V, --verbose

> Display extra progress as RDoc parses.

```
-v, --version
      Print the version.

-h, --help
      Display this help.
```

RubyGems

RubyGems is a package utility for Ruby (*https://rubygems.org*), originally written by Jim Weirich. It installs Ruby software packages, and keeps them up-to-date. It is quite easy to learn and use—even easier than tools like the Unix/Linux `tar` utility (*http://www.gnu.org/software/tar*) or Java's `jar` utility (*http://java.sun.com/j2se/1.5.0/docs/tooldocs/windows/jar.html*).

For more information, read the RubyGems documentation at *http://guides.rubygems.org*. This site provides most everything you need to know about using RubyGems. If you don't have RubyGems installed, go to *https://rubygems.org/pages/download* for installation instructions.

NOTE

You'll find this information on binstubs from Sam Stephenson useful: *https://github.com/sstephenson/rbenv/wiki/Understanding-binstubs*.

Check to see whether RubyGems is installed by typing the following at a shell prompt:

```
$ gem --version
2.4.6
```

Get help on RubyGems:

```
$ gem --help
RubyGems is a sophisticated package manager for
Ruby.  This is a basic help message containing
pointers to more information.
```

```
Usage:
  gem -h/--help
  gem -v/--version
  gem command [arguments...] [options...]

Examples:
  gem install rake
  gem list --local
  gem build package.gemspec
  gem help install

Further help:
  gem help commands            list all 'gem' commands
  gem help examples            show some examples of usage
  gem help gem_dependencies    gem dependencies file guide
  gem help platforms           gem platforms guide
  gem help <COMMAND>           show help on COMMAND
                               (e.g. 'gem help install')
  gem server                   present a web page at
                               http://localhost:8808/
                               with info about installed
gems
  Further information:
    http://guides.rubygems.org
```

Get a list of RubyGems commands by typing:

```
$ gem help commands
```

Get help on a specific RubyGems command, for example, check:

```
$ gem help check
```

Show RubyGems examples:

```
$ gem help examples
```

To list available remote RubyGems packages, use the following (drop the --remote flag to see what you have locally):

```
$ gem list --remote
[truncated — you'll get almost 100,000 gems]
```

Install or update Rake (make à la Ruby, discussed in the next section). You may need root privileges to do this (essentially, you'll need a root password). I use sudo (*http://www.sudo.ws*) to do this:

```
$ sudo gem install rake
```

Rake

A build tool helps you build, compile, or otherwise process files, sometimes large numbers of them. Rake is a build tool like *make* (*http://www.gnu.org/software/make*) and Apache *ant* (*http://ant.apache.org*), but it is written in Ruby. It is used by many Ruby applications, not just Rails. Rails operations use Rake frequently, so it is worth mentioning here.

Rake uses a Rakefile to figure out what to do. A Rakefile contains named tasks. When you create a Rails project, a Rakefile is automatically created to help you deal with a variety of jobs, such as running tests and looking at project statistics. (After creating a Rails project with one of the following tutorials, while in the main Rails project directory, run `rake --tasks` or `rails stats` to get a flavor of what Rake does.)

You'll find information on Rake at *http://docs.seattlerb.org/rake/*. Additionally, you'll find a good introduction to Rake by Martin Fowler at *http://martinfowler.com/articles/rake.html*. Here's the Github repository: *https://github.com/ruby/rake*.

Check to see whether Rake is present:

```
$ rake --version
rake, version 10.4.2
```

If this command fails, use RubyGems to install Rake, as shown in the previous section. RubyGems must be installed first.

To run Rake help, type:

```
$ rake --help
```

The following is displayed:

```
rake [-f rakefile] {options} targets . . .
```

Options:

`--backtrace=[`*OUT*`]`
: Enable full backtrace. `OUT` can be `stderr` (default) or `stdout`.

`--comments`
: Show commented tasks only.

`--job-stats [`*LEVEL*`]`
: Display job statistics. `LEVEL=history` displays a complete job list.

`--rules`
: Trace the rules resolution.

`--suppress-backtrace` *PATTERN*
: Suppress backtrace lines matching regexp `PATTERN`. Ignored if `--trace` is on.

`-A, --all`
: Show all tasks, even uncommented ones (in combination with `-T` or `-D`).

`-B, --build-all`
: Build all prerequisites, including those that are up-to-date.

`-D, --describe [`*PATTERN*`]`
: Describe the tasks (matching optional `PATTERN`), then exit.

`-e, --execute` *CODE*
: Execute some Ruby code and exit.

`-E, --execute-continue` *CODE*
: Execute some Ruby code, and then continue with normal task processing.

`-f, --rakefile [`*FILENAME*`]`
: Use `FILENAME` as the Rakefile to search for.

`-G, --no-system, --nosystem`
: Use standard project Rakefile search paths; ignore system-wide Rakefiles.

-g, --system
> Using system-wide (global) Rakefiles (usually ~/.rake/
> *.rake).

-I, --libdir *LIBDIR*
> Include LIBDIR in the search path for required modules.

-j, --jobs [*NUMBER*]
> Specifies the maximum number of tasks to execute in par-
> allel (default is number of CPU cores + 4).

-m, --multitask
> Treat all tasks as multitasks.

-n, --dry-run
> Do a dry run without executing actions.

-N, --no-search, --nosearch
> Do not search parent directories for the Rakefile.

-P, --prereqs
> Display the tasks and dependencies, and then exit.

-p, --execute-print *CODE*
> Execute some Ruby code, print the result, and then exit.

-q, --quiet
> Do not log messages to standard output.

-r, --require *MODULE*
> Require MODULE before executing Rakefile.

-R, --rakelibdir *RAKELIBDIR*, --rakelib
> Auto-import any *.rake* files in RAKELIBDIR (default is rake
> lib).

-s, --silent
> Like --quiet, but also suppresses the "in directory"
> announcement.

-t, --trace=[*OUT*]
> Turn on invoke/execute tracing, enable full backtrace. OUT
> can be stderr (default) or stdout.

`-T, --tasks [`*`PATTERN`*`]`
> Display the tasks (matching optional `PATTERN`) with descriptions, and then exit.

`-v, --verbose`
> Log message to standard output.

`-V, --version`
> Display the program version.

`-W, --where [`*`PATTERN`*`]`
> Describe the tasks (matching optional `PATTERN`), and then exit.

`-X, --no-deprecation-warnings`
> Disable the deprecation warnings.

`-h, -H, --help`
> Display this help message.

Ruby Resources

- Ruby language main site (*http://www.ruby-lang.org*)
- Matz's blog (in Japanese) (*http://www.rubyist.net/~matz*)
- Ruby documentation (*http://www.ruby-doc.org*)
- Ruby forum (*http://www.ruby-forum.com*)
- Ruby on Rails (*http://www.rubyonrails.org*)
- Rails Conf (*http://railsconf.com*)
- Ruby on Rails blog (*http://weblog.rubyonrails.org*)
- byebug debugger by David Rodríguez (*https://github.com/deivid-rodriguez/byebug*)
- *The Ruby Programming Language* by David Flanagan and Yukihiro Matsumoto (O'Reilly)
- *Programming Ruby 1.9 & 2.0, 4th Edition*, by Dave Thomas, Andy Hunt, and Chad Fowler (Pragmatic Bookshelf)
- *The Ruby Way: Solutions and Techniques in Ruby Programming, 3rd Edition*, by Hal Fulton and André Arko (Addison-Wesley)

- *Why's (Poignant) Guide to Ruby*, by Why the Lucky Stiff (aka Jonathan Gillette)
- *Ruby Cookbook, 2nd Edition*, by Lucas Carlson and Leonard Richardson (O'Reilly)
- *The Well-Grounded Rubyist, 2nd Edition*, by David A. Black (Manning)
- *Ruby in a Nutshell*, by Yukihiro Matsumoto (O'Reilly), which is old but still valuable in many ways (I have a copy signed by the author and still use it often)

Glossary

accessor

A method for accessing data in a class that is usually inaccessible otherwise. Also called getter and setter methods—def a;@a;end and def b=(val);@b=val;end are examples of a getter and setter, respectively. The Module#attr, Module#attr_accessor, Module#attr_reader, and Module#attr_writer metaprogramming methods also define accessors.

aliasing

Using the Ruby keyword alias or Module#alias_method, you can alias a method by specifying a new and old name.

ARGF

An I/O-like stream that allows access to a virtual concatenation of all files provided on the command line, or standard input if no files are provided.

ARGV

An array that contains all of the command-line arguments passed to a program.

argument

The value of a parameter, passed to a method. With the method hello (name), in the call hello ("Matz"), the value "Matz" is the argument. *See also* method.

array

> A data structure containing an ordered list of elements—which can be composed of any Ruby object—starting with an index of 0. *See also* hash.

ASCII

> Abbreviation for American Standard Code for Information Interchange. ASCII is a character set representing 128 letters, numbers, symbols, and special codes, in the range 0–127. Each character can be represented by an 8-bit byte (octet). One of many possible character sets (encodings) now available in Ruby. *See also* UTF-8.

block

> A nameless function, always associated with a method call, contained in a pair of braces ({}) or do/end.

block comment

> *See* comment.

C extensions

> Ruby is actually written in the C programming language. You can extend Ruby with C code, perhaps for performance gains or to do some heavy lifting. *See also* Ruby Inline (*http://www.zenspider.com/projects/rubyinline.html*).

carriage return

> *See* newline.

child class

> A class that is derived from a parent or superclass. *See also* superclass.

class

> A collection of code, including methods and variables, which are called members. The code in a class sets the rules for objects of the given class. *See also* instance, module, object.

class variable

A variable that can be shared between objects of a given class. In Ruby, a class variable is prefixed with two at signs, as in @@count. *See also* global variable, instance variable, local variable.

closure

A nameless function or method. It is like a method within another method that refers to or shares variables with the enclosing or outer method. In Ruby, the closure or block is wrapped by braces ({}) or do/end, and depends on the associated method to do its work. *See also* block.

coding comment

A comment at the start of a Ruby program file that specifies an encoding for the file. For example, # coding: utf-8. *See also* encoding.

comment

Program text that is ignored by the Ruby interpreter. If it is preceded by a #, and not buried in double quotes, the text or line is ignored by the Ruby interpreter. Block comments, enclosed by =begin/=code, can contain comments that cover more than one line. These are also called embedded documents.

composability

The degree to which you can express logic by combining and recombining parts of a language (see "The Design of RELAX NG," by James Clark, at *http://www.thaiopen source.com/relaxng/design.html#section:5*).

concatenation

Joining or chaining together two strings performed in Ruby with the +, <<, and concat methods.

conditional expression

See conditional operator.

conditional operator

An operator that takes three arguments separated by `?` and `:`, a concise form of if/then/else. For example, `label = length == 1 ? " argument" : " arguments"`.

conditional statement

Tests whether a given statement is `true` or `false`, executing code (or not) based on the outcome. Conditional statements are formed with keywords such as `if`, `while`, and `unless`.

constant

In Ruby, a constant name is capitalized or all uppercase. Class names, for example, are constants. A constant is not immutable in Ruby, though when you change the value of a constant, the Ruby interpreter warns you that the constant is already initialized. *See also* variable.

data structure

Data electronically stored in a way that (usually) allows efficient retrieval of the data. Arrays and hashes are examples of data structures.

database

A systematic collection of information, stored on a computer. Ruby on Rails is an example of a database-enabled web application framework.

default

A value that is assigned automatically when interacting with code or a program.

delegation

Delegation in object-oriented programming is, basically, the delegation of tasks from one object to another helper object. See `BasicObject#method_missing`. Ruby also has a delegator library. See *http://ruby-doc.org/stdlib-2.2.2/libdoc/delegate/rdoc/Delegator.html*.

each

> In Ruby, a method named `each` (or named similarly, like `each_line`) iterates over a given block, processing the data piece by piece—by bytes, characters, lines, elements, and so forth, depending on the structure of the data. *See also* block.

embedded document

> *See* comment.

embedded Ruby

> *See* ERB.

enumerable

> In Ruby, the `Enumerable` module provides collection classes with methods for traversal, search, and sort capability. See *http://ruby-doc.org/core-2.2.2/Enumerable.html*.

enumerator

> In Ruby, an *enumerator* is an `Enumerable` object that enumerates or lists some other object. *See also* enumerable.

error

> A problem or defect in code that usually causes a program to halt. Common errors in Ruby programs are identified with classes such as `ArgumentError`, `EOFError`, and `ZeroDivisionError`. *See also* exception.

ERB

> An abbreviation for *eRuby* (*embedded Ruby*). A technique, similar to JavaServer Pages, for embedding Ruby code in tags—such as `<%=` and `%>`—in text files, including HTML and XHTML, which is executed when the files are processed. Ruby on Rails makes extensive use of embedded Ruby. ERB is part of Ruby's standard library (see *http://ruby-doc.org/stdlib-2.2.2/libdoc/erb/rdoc/index.html*), but other implementations also exist, such as Erubis (*http://www.kuwata-lab.com/erubis*) and ember (*http://snk.tuxfamily.org/lib/ember/*).

encoding

> Since 1.9, Ruby has offered built-in Unicode support and other multibyte text representations as well. In addition, it added the --encoding (-E) command-line switch, magic or coding comments, and eliminated the -K switch and the predefined variable $KCODE. Classes such as String and Regexp are now encoding-aware.

eRuby

> *See* ERB.

exception

> Allows you to catch and manage runtime and other errors while programming. Managed with rescue, ensure, and raise. *See also* error.

expression

> A programming statement that returns a value and includes keywords, operators, variables, and so forth.

expression substitution

> In Ruby, a syntax that allows you to embed expressions in strings and other contexts. The substitution is enclosed in #{ and }, and the result of the expression replaces the substitution in place when the code runs via the Ruby interpreter. This is also called *string interpolation*. You can also perform string interpolation with Kernel#printf, IO#printf, and Kernel#sprintf.

extension, file

> The part of the filename (if present) that follows a period (RHS). The conventional file extension for Ruby is *.rb*.

extension, C

> *See* C extensions.

file mode

> Depending on how it is set, determines the ability to read, write, and execute a file. One way to set a file's mode is with File.new at the time of file creation.

---

float

In Ruby, objects that represent real numbers, such as 1.0. A floating-point number in Ruby is an instance of the Float class.

gem

See RubyGems.

general delimited strings

A technique for creating strings using %! and !, where ! can be an arbitrary non-alphanumeric character. Alternative syntax: %Q!string! for double-quoted strings, %q!string! for single-quoted strings, and %x!string! for back quoted strings.

getter method

A method that "gets" the value of an instance variable, for example, def a;@a;end. *See also* accessor, setter method.

garbage collection

Garbage collection, or GC, in Ruby automatically destroys unneeded, unreachable objects, making programs less likely to spring memory links. The GC module offers several methods that manage garbage collection explicitly. See *http://ruby-doc.org/core-2.2.2/GC.html*. *See also* Object Space::garbage_collect.

GC

See garbage collection.

Git

Git is a popular, distributed version control system that quickly and efficiently handles coding projects large and small. *See* GitHub.

GitHub

GitHub is a popular, online Git repository that offers the functionality of Git as well as its own special features. *See also* Git.

global variable

A variable whose scope includes the entire program. Can be done with a singleton. *See also* class variable, instance variable, local variable, singleton.

graphical user interface

See GUI.

GUI

An abbreviation for *graphical user interface*. A user interface that focuses on graphics rather than text. Tcl/Tk is Ruby's built-in GUI library.

hash

An unordered collection of data where keys are mapped to values. *See also* array, hash code.

hash code

An integer calculated from an object. Identical objects have the same hash code. Generated by a hash method. *See also* hash.

here document

A technique that allows you to build strings from multiple lines, using <<*name*/*name* where *name* is an arbitrary name. Alternative syntax: <<"*string*"/*string* for double-quoted strings, <<'*string*'/*string* for single-quoted strings, <<'*string*'/*string* for back quoted strings, and <<-*string*/*string* for indented strings.

hexadecimal

A base-16 number, represented by the digits 0–9 and the letters A–F or a–f. Often prefixed with 0x. For example, the base-10 number 26 is represented as 0x1A in hexadecimal.

index

An integer that numbers or identifies the elements in an array. Array indexes always start with 0. *See also* array.

inheritance

The ability of a class to inherit features from another class via the < operator. *See also* multiple inheritance, single inheritance.

instance

An object that is created when a class is instantiated, often with new class method; for example, str = String.new creates str, an instance of the String class.

instance variable

A variable associated with an instance of a class. In Ruby, instance variables are prefixed with a single at sign—for example, @name. *See also* class variable, local variable, global variable.

I/O

An abbreviation for *input/output*. Refers to the flow of data to and from a computing device, such as reading data to and from a file. The IO class is the basis for all of Ruby's I/O, and the File class is a subclass of IO.

key

A key is associated with a value in a hash data structure. You use keys to access hash values. *See also* hash.

keyword

A special word used in programming syntax, such as class or def in Ruby. Also called a *reserved word*.

lambda

In Ruby, a Kernel method that expects a block and returns a Proc object. This object is a lambda, not a proc. It is bound to the current context and does parameter checking (checks the number of them) when called. *See also* block, proc.

library

See standard library.

line-end character

    See newline.

linefeed

    See newline.

local variable

    3009.40A variable with local scope, such as inside a method. You cannot access a local variable from outside of its scope. In Ruby, local variables begin with a lowercase letter or an underscore (_). `num` and `_outer` are examples of local variables. *See also* class variable, global variable, instance variable.

loop

    A repeatable iteration of one or more programming statements. Ruby uses `for` loops, and even has a `Kernel#loop` method for such a task. A loop may be stopped (with `break`). Control then passes to the next statement in the program, to a special location, or it may exit the program.

magic comments

    See coding comment.

main

    The initial, top-level execution context for Ruby programs. Test it by entering `self` in *irb*.

match

    When a method finds its specified regular expression, it is said to match. *See also* regular expression.

member

    Variables and methods are considered members of a class or object. *See also* class, method, object, variable.

metaprogramming

    Programming that creates and/or manipulates other programs. Ruby's `define_method` method is an important tool that can be used in metaprogramming. Reflection is another capability that plays a role in metaprogramming. *See also* reflection.

method

A named collection of statements, with or without arguments, that returns a value (either explicitly or implicitly). A method is a member of a class. *See also* class.

mixin

When a module is included in a class, it is mixed into the class, hence the name *mixin*. Using mixins helps avoid issues that can arise from multiple inheritance. *See also* module.

mode, file

See file mode.

module

A module is like a class but cannot be instantiated like a class. A class can include a module so that when the class is instantiated, it gets the included module's methods and so forth. The methods from an included module become instance methods in the class that includes the module. This is called mixing in, and a module is referred to as a mixin. *See also* class, mixin.

modulo

A division operation that returns the remainder of the operation. The percent sign (%) is used as the modulo operator.

multiple inheritance

When a class can inherit more than one class. C++, for example, supports multiple inheritance, which has disadvantages (such as name collision) that, in many opinions, outweigh the advantages. *See also* single inheritance.

name collision

Names (identifiers) collide when they cannot be resolved unambiguously. This is a risk of multiple inheritance.

namespace

In Ruby, a module acts as a namespace. A namespace is a set of names—such as method names—that have a scope or context. A Ruby module associates a single name with a set of method and constant names. The module name can be used in classes in other modules. Generally, the scope or context of such a namespace is the class or module where the namespace (module name) is included. A Ruby class can also be considered a namespace.

newline

A character that ends a line, such as a linefeed (Mac OS X and Unix/Linux) or a combination of characters such as character return and linefeed (Windows).

nil

Empty, uninitialized, or invalid. `nil` is always `false`, but is not the same as zero. It is an object of `NilClass`.

object

An instance of a class, a thing, an entity, or a concept that is represented in contiguous memory in a computer. *See also* instance, class.

object-oriented programming

A programming practice based on organizing data with methods that can manipulate that data. The methods and data (members) are organized into classes that can be instantiated as objects. *See also* class.

octal

A base-8 number, represented by the digits 0–7. Often prefixed with 0 [zero]. The decimal number `026` (note prefix) is 32 in octal, for example. You can enter octal digits in a string in the form `\onnn` where *n* is a digit. This form can take one to three digits in the ranges 0 to 7, 00 to 77, and 000 and 377, respectively.

OOP

See object-oriented programming.

---

operators

> *Operators* perform operations, such as addition, subtraction, multiplication, and division. Ruby operators include, like other languages, + for addition, - for subtraction, * for multiplication, / for division, % for modulo, and so forth. Many Ruby operators are methods (that can be overridden).

overloading

> Method or function overloading is a practice in object-oriented programming that allows methods with the same name to operate on different kinds of data (methods or functions with the same name but different signatures). You can't really overload methods in Ruby without branching the logic inside the method. *See also* overriding.

overriding

> Redefining a method. The latest definition is the one recognized by the Ruby interpreter. *See also* overloading.

package

> *See* RubyGems.

parent class

> *See* superclass.

path

> The location of a file on a filesystem. Used to help locate files for opening, executing, and so forth. Contained in the PATH environment variable.

pattern

> A sequence of ordinary and special characters that enables a regular expression engine to locate a string. *See also* regular expression.

pop

> A term related to a stack—a last-in, first-out (LIFO) data structure. When you pop an element off a stack, you are

removing the last element first. You can pop elements off (out of) an array in Ruby. *See also* push.

push

A term related to a stack—a last-in, first-out (LIFO) data structure. When you push an element onto a stack, you are adding an element onto the end of the array. You can push elements onto an array in Ruby. *See also* pop.

precision

Refers to the preciseness with which a numerical quantity is expressed. The Precision module in Ruby enables you to convert numbers (float to integer, integer to float).

private

A method that is marked private can only be accessed, or is only visible, within its own class. *See also* protected, public.

proc

In Ruby, a procedure that is stored as an object, complete with context; an object of the Proc class. *See also* lambda.

protected

A method that is marked protected can only be accessed or visible within its own class, or from within child classes. *See also* private, public.

public

A method that is marked public (which is the default) is accessible or visible in its own class and from other classes. *See also* private, protected.

RDoc

A tool for generating documentation embedded in comments in Ruby source code. See *https://github.com/rdoc/rdoc* and *http://docs.seattlerb.org/rdoc*.

Rails

See also Ruby on Rails.

Rake

A build tool written in Ruby with capabilities like make. See *http://docs.seattlerb.org/rake/* and *https://github.com/ruby/rake*.

random number

With the Kernel#rand or Kernel#srand methods, Ruby can generate an arbitrary, pseudorandom number.

range

In Ruby, a way of representing inclusive (..) and exclusive (...) ranges of objects, usually numbers. For example, 1..10 is a range of numbers from 1 to 10, inclusive; using ... instead of .. excludes the last value from the range.

rational number

A fraction. In Ruby, rational numbers are handled via the Rational class.

RoR

Abbreviation for Ruby on Rails. *See* Ruby on Rails.

receiver

An object that receives or is the context for the action that a method performs. In the method call *str*.length, *str* is the receiver of the length method.

reflection

The ability of a language such as Ruby to examine and manipulate itself. For example, the reflection method class from Object returns an object's class.

regular expression

A concise sequence or pattern of ordinary and special characters used to match strings. *See also* match.

reserved word

See keyword.

RubyForge

Was web-based archive for Ruby applications that shut down in 2014.

RubyGems

The premier packing system for Ruby applications. A RubyGems package is called a `gem`. It comes with Ruby (though you can choose to install it explicitly).

Ruby on Rails

A popular, open source web application framework written in Ruby. It was first released in 2004 and, at the time of writing, was at version 4.2. It follows the model-view-controller, or MVC, architectural pattern. Matz once called it Ruby's killer app. See *http://rubyonrails.org*.

self

`self` represents the current object or receiver invoked by a method. *See also* receiver.

setter method

A method that "sets" the value of an instance variable; for example, def b=(val);@b=val;end. *See also* accessor, getter method.

single inheritance

When a class can inherit from only one class, as opposed to multiple classes where a class may inherit from multiple classes. *See also* multiple inheritance.

singleton

A singleton class is tied to a particular object, can be instantiated only once, and is not distinguished by a pre-fixed name. A singleton method is tied to the `Singleton` class. May be used like or in place of a class variable.

standard library

A library or collection of Ruby code containing packages that perform specialized tasks. Some example packages are REXML for XML processing, and Iconv for character set conversion. Online documentation is available at *http://ruby-doc.org/stdlib*.

statement

An instruction for a program to carry out.

string

A sequence of objects, usually symbols of human-readable characters.

string interpolation

See expression substitution.

substitution

See expression substitution.

superclass

The parent class. A child class is derived from the parent or superclass. *See also* child class.

Tcl/Tk

The Tcl scripting language with the Tk user interface toolkit is provided in Ruby's standard library.

ternary operator

See conditional operator.

thread

Ruby supports threading. Threading allows programs to execute multiple tasks simultaneously (or almost simultaneously) by slicing the time on the clock that runs the computer processor. The threads in Ruby are operating-system independent, so threading is available on all platforms that run Ruby, even if the OS doesn't support them.

Unicode

An international character coding system that allows 65,000 or more characters. You can enter Unicode characters in a string (using UTF-8 encoding) in the form \u*xxxx* in the range 0000 and FFFF (you can't drop leading zeros), or \u{*xxxxxx*} in the range 0 and 10FFFF (you can drop

leading zeros), or multiple codepoints in the form
\u{*xxxxxx[xxxxxx . . .]*} (one to six hexadecimal digits, separated by spaces or tabs). *See http://
www.unicode.org.*

UTF-8

A character set, based on one to four bytes, that can
describe most characters in human writing systems. Set
with --encoding or -E. *See also* ASCII.

variable

An identifier or name that may be assigned to an object
which in turn may hold a quantity or a value. *See also* class
variable, global variable, instance variable, local variable.

XML

An abbreviation for *Extensible Markup Language*. A language specified by the W3C (*http://www.w3c.org*) that
enables you to create vocabularies using elements and
other markup. Ruby uses REXML, Builder, and libxml to
process XML.

Index

Symbols

! (exclamation mark)
  != (not equal to) operator, 18
  !~ (not match) operator, 18,
    106
  logical negation operator, 17,
    42
  method names ending in, 34
(hash character)
  #! shebang line, 7, 12
  in Ruby comments, 19
$ (dollar sign)
  $ predefined variable, 26, 27
  $! predefined variable, 25
  $$ predefined variable, 27
  $& predefined variable, 26
  $* predefined variable, 27
  $+ predefined variable, 26
  $, output field separator
    between arguments, 27
  $-0 predefined variable, 28
  $-a predefined variable, 28
  $-d predefined variable, 28
  $-F predefined variable, 28
  $-i predefined variable, 29
  $-I predefined variable, 29
  $-l predefined variable, 29

$-p predefined variable, 29
$-v predefined variable, 29
$-w predefined variable, 29
$. predefined variable, 27
$/ predefined variable, 26
$0 predefined variable, 27
$1, $2... predefined variable,
  26
$: predefined variable, 27
$; predefined variable, 27
$< predefined variable, 27
$= predefined variable, 26
$> predefined variable, 27
$? predefined variable, 27
$@ predefined variable, 25
$DEBUG predefined variable,
  28
$FILENAME predefined vari-
  able, 28
$LOADED_FEATURES pre-
  defined variable, 28
$LOAD_PATH predefined
  variable, 28, 59
$stderr predefined variable,
  28, 70
$stdin predefined variable, 28,
  70

About the Author

Michael Fitzgerald is an author, coder, and novelist who has written over 20 books. In addition to English, his technical works have been translated into Spanish, Portuguese, French, German, Polish, Korean, Japanese, and Chinese. When he's not writing, he likes to spend time on skis, riding horses, running, and with his family. You can connect with him at *michaeljames fitzgerald.com*.

Colophon

The animals on the cover of *Ruby Pocket Reference* are giraffes (*Giraffa camelopardalis*), the tallest of all land animals. A giraffe can reach 16 to 18 feet in height and weigh up to 3,000 pounds. Its species name, camelopardalis, is derived from an early Roman name, which described the giraffe as resembling both a camel and a leopard. The spots that cover its body act as camouflage in the African savanna. Its long neck and tough, prehensile tongue allow it to feed in treetops, consuming about 140 pounds of leaves and twigs daily. And its complex cardiovascular system and 24-pound heart regulate circulation throughout its tremendous body: in the upper neck, a pressure-regulation system prevents excess blood flow to the brain when the giraffe lowers its head to drink, while thick sheaths of skin on the lower legs maintain high extravascular pressure to compensate for the weight of the fluid pressing down on them.

Giraffes travel in herds comprised of about a dozen females, one or two males, and their young. Other males may travel alone, in pairs, or in bachelor herds. Male giraffes determine female fertility by tasting the female's urine to detect estrus. Yet sexual relations in male giraffes are most frequently homosexual: the proportion of same-sex courtships varies between 30 and 75 percent. Among females, homosexual mounting appears to comprise only 1 percent of all incidents. Gestation lasts between 14 and 15 months, after which a single calf is born. Only 25 to 50 percent of calves reach adulthood, as the giraffe's predators—including lions, leopards, hyenas, and African wild dogs—mainly prey on young.

Giraffes use their long necks and keen sense of smell, hearing, and eyesight to guard against attacks. They can reach speeds of up to 30 miles per hour and fight off predators using their muscular hind legs. A single kick from an adult giraffe can shatter a lion's skull. Giraffes were once hunted for their skin and tail but are currently a protected species.

Many of the animals on O'Reilly covers are endangered; all of them are important to the world. To learn more about how you can help, go to *animals.oreilly.com*.

The cover image is from loose plates (original source unknown). The cover fonts are URW Typewriter and Guardian Sans. The text font is Adobe Minion Pro; the heading font is Adobe Myriad Condensed; and the code font is Dalton Maag's Ubuntu Mono.

Get even more for your money.

Join the O'Reilly Community, and register the O'Reilly books you own. It's free, and you'll get:

- $4.99 ebook upgrade offer
- 40% upgrade offer on O'Reilly print books
- Membership discounts on books and events
- Free lifetime updates to ebooks and videos
- Multiple ebook formats, DRM FREE
- Participation in the O'Reilly community
- Newsletters
- Account management
- 100% Satisfaction Guarantee

Signing up is easy:

1. Go to: oreilly.com/go/register
2. Create an O'Reilly login.
3. Provide your address.
4. Register your books.

Note: English-language books only

To order books online:
oreilly.com/store

For questions about products or an order:
orders@oreilly.com

To sign up to get topic-specific email announcements and/or news about upcoming books, conferences, special offers, and new technologies:
elists@oreilly.com

For technical questions about book content:
booktech@oreilly.com

To submit new book proposals to our editors:
proposals@oreilly.com

O'Reilly books are available in multiple DRM-free ebook formats. For more information:
oreilly.com/ebooks

O'REILLY®

A *flip-flop expression* is an obscure use of a range operator. For example, (1..7).each {|n| p n if n==2..n>=5} prints 2 through 5. A flip-flop expression is false until the expression on the left evaluates to true. It remains true until the expression on the right evaluates to true, and then goes back to false. Got that? Flip-flops came to Ruby by way of Perl, *sed*, and *awk*. They should generally be avoided but are worth a mention for the intrepid out there who will use them all the time.

Methods

Methods provide a way to collect and organize program statements and expressions into one place so that you can use them conveniently and repeatedly. Most of Ruby's operators are actually methods. Here is a simple definition of a method named hello, created with the keywords def and end:

```
def hello
  puts "Hello, world!"
end
```

When you invoke the method hello, it outputs or emits a string:

```
hello # => Hello, world!
```

You can undefine a method with undef:

```
undef hello # undefines the method named hello
hello # try calling this method now
NameError: undefined local variable or method
  'hello' for main:Object
```

Methods might or might not have parameters. The repeat method, inane as it is, takes two parameters, word and times:

```
def repeat( word, times )
  puts word * times
end
```

```
repeat("Hello! ", 3) # => Hello! Hello! Hello!
repeat "Goodbye! ", 4 # => Goodbye! Goodbye!
  Goodbye! Goodbye!
```

Parentheses are optional in most Ruby method definitions and calls; however, if you call a method within a method—a nested call—it might cause some confusion, both on the part of the coder and the Ruby interpreter. When using parentheses, keep in mind that the opening parenthesis must follow the method name with no intervening space.

For more information, see *http://ruby-doc.org/core-2.2.2/doc/syntax/methods_rdoc.html*.

For the purposes of this book, *parameters* are part of the method definition or signature, and *arguments* are the values passed by those parameters. I say this because sometimes parameters and arguments are used interchangeably.

You may join an object and its method with either :: or ., but usually :: is used with class methods. You may also use # with instance methods.

Block Arguments

Blocks are namelessly passed to their associated methods. However, you can pass blocks to methods directly by using a *block argument*, which essentially turns them into named blocks. (No exception is generated if the block is not passed.) The block parameter must be the last parameter in the method definition and must be prefixed with an ampersand, as in &. Because the value of the block argument is actually a Proc object, you have to use the Proc#call method rather than yield to process the block. Here's a sample (*block_arg.rb*):

```
def my_iterator(x, &b)
  i = 0
```